CASHUP DAVIS

CASHUP DAVIS

THE INSPIRING LIFE OF A
SECRET MENTOR

JEFF BURNSIDE

INVESTIGATIVE JOURNALIST

and

GORDON W. DAVIS

GREAT-GRANDSON

BASALT BOOKS

PULLMAN, WASHINGTON

BASALT BOOKS

Basalt Books
PO Box 645910
Pullman, Washington 99164-5910
Phone: 800-354-7360
Email: basalt.books@wsu.edu
Website: basaltbooks.wsu.edu

Library of Congress Cataloging-in-Publication Data

Names: Burnside, Jeff, author. | Davis, G. W., author.
Title: Cashup Davis : the inspiring life of a secret mentor / Jeff
Burnside, investigative journalist, and Gordon W. Davis, great-grandson.
Description: Pullman, Washington : Basalt Books, [2022] | Includes
bibliographical references.
Identifiers: LCCN 2022033441 | ISBN 9781638640059 (paperback)
Subjects: LCSH: Davis, James S., 1815-1896. | Pioneers--Washington
(State)--Whitman County--Biography. | Hotels--Washington
(State)--Whitman County--History--19th century. |
Businesspeople--Washington (State)--Whitman County--Biography. | Davis
family. | Whitman County (Wash.)--History--19th century. | Whitman
County (Wash.)--Biography.
Classification: LCC F897.W6 B87 2022 | DDC 979.7/03092
[B]--dc23/eng/20220722
LC record available at https://lccn.loc.gov/2022033441

Basalt Books is an imprint of Washington State University Press.

The Washington State University Pullman campus is located on the homelands
of the Niimíipuu (Nez Perce) Tribe and the Palus people. We acknowledge their
presence here since time immemorial and recognize their continuing connection to
the land, to the water, and to their ancestors. WSU Press is committed to publishing
works that foster a deeper understanding of the Pacific Northwest and the contribu-
tions of its Native peoples.

Cover design by Jeffry A. Hipp
Interior design by Hannah Gaskamp

CONTENTS

FOREWORD   ix

PROLOGUE: THE JOURNEY   xi

1   FIRE IN THE NIGHT SKY   1

2   CASTLES IN THE AIR   8

3   ADVENTURE IN AMERICA   16

4   MARY ANN SAYS "NO MORE"   45

5   THE SETTLERS AND THE INDIANS   64

6   THE STAGE STOP AND THE ADVENT OF
    "CASHUP"   77

7   THE PALOUSE BECOMES RENOWNED   90

8   THE HOTEL ON THE HILL   109

9   THE GRAND OPENING   127

10 WHEN MARY ANN DIED   144

11 DARK HALLWAYS   151

12 CASHUP'S GREATEST ACHIEVEMENT
    AND GREATEST FAILURE   169

EPILOGUE: LIFE LESSONS FROM THE
    MOUNTAINTOP   185

APPENDIX: SETTLERS OF THE PALOUSE   195

SOURCES   203

ACKNOWLEDGEMENTS
    FROM JEFF BURNSIDE   207

ACKNOWLEDGEMENTS
    FROM GORDON DAVIS   211

ABOUT THE AUTHORS   213

Our book is dedicated to the hundreds of Cashup Davis descendants living across America, including Washington, Oregon, Idaho, California, Texas, Arizona, Iowa, Wisconsin, and Ohio, and those residing in the United Kingdom and beyond.

PRAISE FOR *CASHUP DAVIS*:

"It's not easy to capture the full measure of one's life, but the authors have done just that in writing this book"—Lawrence Schovanec, President, Texas Tech University

"Cashup Davis was a tireless visionary, one of those Western pioneers whose unbounded energy helped build a nation. His life story is a tale of castles in the air and of real, stirring achievement."—David Baron, author of *American Eclipse* and *The Beast in the Garden*

"What a story! With lucid writing and illuminating detail culled from historical and family documents, they tell a compelling story as unusual as their subject's name."—Tom Yulsman, Director of the Center for Environmental Journalism at the University of Colorado Boulder

"The life of Cashup Davis—pioneer, dreamer, big thinker, risk taker, and entrepreneur—whose actions and mindset influenced his great-grandson and surely will influence you."—Dr. Kevin R. Pond, Dean of the Paul Engler College of Agriculture and Natural Sciences, West Texas A&M University

"We loved it! At a time when the world can use an inspirational story, along comes an uplifting winner in the little-known story of Cashup Davis."—Gerald Posner, author of *PHARMA* and *Case Closed*, and Trisha Posner, author of *The Pharmacist of Auschwitz*

"A firsthand account of how to be an achiever against incredible obstacles…gritty and tough, just like they like it in the eastern Washington Palouse. You will be inspired."—Mike Leach, former head football coach, Washington State University, bestselling author, *Swing Your Sword, Geronimo,* and *Sports for Dorks: Football*

"I know how hard it is to be an entrepreneur, overcoming obstacles and chasing your dreams. I see the same thing in Cashup. It's a page turner."—Rob Angel, creator of Pictionary, author of *Game Changer*

FOREWORD

ELIZABETH S. CHILTON

PROVOST AND PROFESSOR OF ANTHROPOLOGY

CHANCELLOR, WASHINGTON STATE UNIVERSITY PULLMAN

THIS BOOK IS THE AMAZING story of the life of James "Cashup" Davis—his travels, his adventures, his business ventures, and his family. It is also a snapshot into the history of Euro-American westward expansion during the nineteenth century. Whether or not the reader has been to the Palouse, where Cashup spent the latter part of his life, this book brings to life what it was like to try to find a piece of earth to farm, make your fortune, and provide for your family through your own tenacity and fortitude.

One quality of Cashup's that comes across very clearly is that, as the authors put it, he had "no interest in mediocrity." It is clear he held himself and others to a high standard and had an inordinate amount of determination—far beyond simple ambition. Anyone who has hiked or driven up to the top of Steptoe Butte and taken in the amazing vista will appreciate the drive (or, dare I say, hubris!) of the man who, at that time, would build an enormous hotel at the top of that impressive geological feature.

The book also probes the question: what is one's true legacy? Early on in Cashup's life, he was clearly focused on the survival and stability of his family. In later years, Cashup was fixated on the act of achievement itself, which secondarily brought him wealth. But even though he may not have realized it, his true legacy is not the wealth he acquired or the large hotel that became a major social and commercial hub in eastern Washington. His legacy is the drive to succeed and commitment to family he passed down to his family through the generations. Gordon Davis, co-author of this book, refers to Cashup (his great-grandfather) as his "secret mentor." Gordon Davis' own life, as we discover in these pages, is an inspiring story of true grit and extraordinary success. This book is a rousing homage to a man who left a strong legacy. But it is also a riveting exploration of how a family's heritage can inform present generations, and how history can inspire generations to come.

Steptoe Butte towers imposingly above the surrounding farms. Photograph by Jon Jonckers.

THE JOURNEY

GORDON W. DAVIS

Don't go to your grave with a life unused.
FOOTBALL COACHING LEGEND BOBBY BOWDEN

CASHUP DAVIS IS MY SECRET mentor. He can be yours too. Cashup is timeless, and so are the lessons I have learned from his extraordinary life. I never met him; he died nearly half a century before I was born. But the more I find out about him, the more inspired I become.

And Cashup is one helluva story.

This is a true story, a "chase your dreams" story. It is an underdog story, an immigrant story, a compelling history. It is an "are you kidding me?!" story, and a story about the pursuit of excellence. Cashup had no interest in mediocrity or doing things halfway. This is also a story about how we define success, a pressing issue for today. Cashup thought he knew what success looked like. He also thought he knew what his legacy would be. He may have been wrong on both counts, and we can all learn from it.

My first awareness of Cashup was as a boy in the 1950s riding in a farm truck with my father Aubrey, Cashup's grandson. As we drove around the magnificent rolling hills of the Palouse farmland in America's Pacific Northwest, Dad would point out majestic Steptoe Butte, rising out of the surrounding wheat fields like a sentinel. "You know," my dad would often say, "Cashup built a grand hotel way up there on the top of Steptoe Butte in 1888, at age 72." I would look to the summit and admire Cashup's audacity. Growing up, my dad shared many more Cashup stories with me. And when relatives got together, it was really Cashup time. He was always spoken about with reverence and respect. We marveled at this ancestor of ours, and his accomplished descendants, with great pride.

I became more curious about Cashup as I read about him in newspaper articles over the years and particularly in 1967 when I read the late Randall Johnson's nineteen-page booklet about him. Cashup died in 1896 and yet, more than 125 years later, people still write about him. I wanted to learn more. With Jeff Burnside's lead, I wanted to investigate, preserve, and share a complete account of my great-grandfather's life, to provide inspiration not just for descendants but for everyone. After all, as one of his great-grandchildren, I possess 12.5% of his genes. With Jeff's help, I take a deeper dive into the legacy of Cashup Davis.

Cashup was a puny kid with a quick smile and a brilliant mind in 1800s England when he got the bug for the American West. He could not shake it. He left everything and came not just to America but to the very edge of western settlement—a region everyone in the civilized world was hearing about. The "quest" characteristic drove him to do something incredible. Yet, in the end, even Cashup misjudged his own legacy. Examining the true definition of success is a life lesson for all of us.

He has served as an inspiration for me. He was determined to go after his amazing, half-crazy dreams, despite the challenges. And there were many. I am guessing you have some big dreams too. Just like Cashup, you are going to hit a few roadblocks. More than one person is going to tell you (or already has) you are unwise to go after your particular dream. I have been there, too.

Cashup did not listen to his detractors; nor should you (although I advise you to read closely the caveats in this cautionary tale of ambition and dreams).

Sure, Cashup's genes are a major part of my DNA. And the more I learn about him, the more I see him in me. Cashup and I are both determined, impatient, driven, a bit gruff on the outside, but have a big heart on the inside. And we both like cigars and a good time. Yet, Cashup is there for everyone, not just for direct descendants like me.

I am blessed in that I have experienced and achieved much in my life: growing up on two farms, four college degrees, twenty-one years of teaching, a wonderful family, academic achievement, a business I founded in 1984 (CEV Multimedia) that has helped revolutionize classroom instruction by transforming textbooks to media-rich online content and now, I am proud to say, provides 22,000 teachers and 1.3 million students with online instructional resources across all fifty states and various countries. Such success required significant risk and extremely hard work to achieve, satisfaction for a job well done that I proudly share with current and former CEV colleagues, students, and collaborators. Just prior to publication of this book, I sold my company, now named iCEV, to The Riverside Company, a terrific enterprise. Conditions for the deal included the retention of all employees, our brand, and our home base in Lubbock, Texas. Integrity is important to me, as it was for Cashup, in all business transactions (small or large) and interactions with others. If people are dishonest in their personal lives, you can bet they carry that into their business dealings.

Additionally, I have become even more philanthropic. Since 2005, we have made significant donations, primarily to six universities, to our family foundation, and to various charitable organizations. Supporting good causes brings both my wife Joyce and me a satisfaction which runs profoundly deep. Since 2005, we have learned that the more we give, the luckier we get. Good advice for anyone.

Gordon Davis holds a top hat that once belonged to his great-grandfather Cashup Davis, and stands alongside the telescope from Cashup's hotel on Steptoe Butte. Photograph by Childress Photography Group, Lubbock, TX.

Yet, an unanswered question ripples through me: Why am I so fortunate? Why did this universe pick me for success? What did I really do to deserve the opportunity for my wife and me in 2020 to establish the Gordon and Joyce Davis Foundation? Did

I deserve it when Texas Tech University named their meat science laboratory after me in 2006 or when in 2022 administrators changed the name of the College of Agricultural Sciences and Natural Resources to the Davis College?

I think the partial answer is found in Cashup Davis, one of thirty-five real-life mentors I have had in my life. This book is my journey to find those answers and to find out about Cashup. I hope you will find some answers in ol' Cashup too. His inspiration is there for the taking.

Award-winning investigative journalist Jeff Burnside and I dug deep. In the archives of small-town museums—musty boxes, file folders, microfilm. Via cemetery visits and scouring burial records. Using drones. Investigating back roads. Sifting through countless newspaper articles and family records. We searched obscure digital archives, mining for nuggets about the Palouse Country of Eastern Washington, the American Midwest, and New York Harbor, and we explored digital archives about Hastings at the southern tip of England. We trod through the best wheat fields in the world. We even put up posters in farm towns around the Palouse that asked anyone walking by: "Is Cashup Davis in your attic?" In so doing, we invited people to check their family trunks and bring items to community meetings in the hopes of finding more photos, documents, letters, and artifacts that would give us further insight into Cashup and his story. Eventually Jeff formed The Cashup Crew, an informal squad of people listed at the end of this book—people who were interested in unearthing as much as we could about Cashup. And it worked.

In the following pages, we will take you along on my unfolding journey. Remember, it can be your journey, too. Start your own legacy or continue what you have already begun.

After all, a little Cashup probably exists in all of us.

ONE

FIRE IN THE NIGHT SKY

A people without the knowledge of their past history, origin and culture is like a tree without roots.

MARCUS GARVEY, JOURNALIST

NO ONE HAD EVER SEEN anything like it.

The calm of a mild spring evening in 1911 brought a hush to the undulating hills of the Palouse region in the young state of Washington. The sun had set several hours earlier and a nearly cloudless sky that night brought out the stars over the farming town of Oakesdale, in Whitman County. Fifty-four-year-old Ferdinand (Ferd) Davis, a stocky man who lived a few miles outside the town where he had been postmaster a few years back as well as president of the local bank, had just settled in after a day of relaxation, church, and his wife Mimi's Sunday home cooking.

Ferd farmed 3,000 acres on the Palouse with his fifteen-year-old son Barber. His wheat fields were shocked with green stocks rising skyward, waiting for summer harvest of golden crops in some of the most fertile soil settlers had ever seen. After a week of hard work on the farm, the two took in a day of rest and peacefulness.

Until the phone rang. Telephone lines, installed with the help of his family, were still a bit new, so any ring was a little jolting. But this time, a panicked caller implored Ferd to look to the horizon.

FIRE!

It was March 15, a day when the remnants of a dream were going up in flames.

What had once been a grand hotel perched at the top of Steptoe Butte, jutting more than a thousand feet above the surrounding farms, was a fiercely raging inferno. The hotel had been boarded up for nearly a decade and left to wildlife, hikers, and mischievous kids. But now it was aflame.

The fire was so big, so intense, that flames licked the night sky, illuminating the growing pillar of smoke racing toward the heavens. Steptoe Butte was by far one of the highest points on the Palouse and could be seen for miles around.

Once Ferd pulled his eyes away from the fire on the butte, he scrambled for his telescope, likely one of very few throughout the region and certainly one of the finest, most powerful telescopes in the Pacific Northwest. It had been in the Davis family for many years, purchased by his father, James "Cashup" Davis. Ferd spun the telescope toward the south, giving him the best—and the most horrific—view of the blaze.

Once Ferd locked in the sightline and his eye focused onto the flames, well, it was enough to make a grown man audibly gasp.

Indeed, this was not just any hotel. For several years in its heyday, after opening July 4, 1888, it was the grandest one around—dreamt of, conceived, built, and run by his eccentric and charismatic father. Cashup Davis had been a well-known businessman, farmer, rancher, and pioneer and one of the most renowned party hosts anywhere in the region. When he walked into a town, people often gathered around him. His visits made news. He earned his nickname by insisting on paying—and on being paid—in cash, a story we will delve into later.

At a time when the region was only sparsely populated with white settlers, Cashup created such a stir with his hotel, his promotional genius, and his gatherings that patrons came from miles around on horseback and in wagons to party, dance, eat, and enjoy life. They had so much fun, ate so much exotic food, and drank so much liquor at the hotel that, given the inconvenient and harrowing return route down the butte, many of them rented rooms to stay until morning. Of course, it was not uncommon for folks to return home the next day without any sleep at all.

Imagine: at a time when almost all of Cashup's guests were accustomed to homes built only of simple planking—sometimes even sod or logs—his elaborate three-story building inspired them to venture for miles, wind up a steep hill, and enter. The structure must have seemed fantastical to the farmers, ranchers, loggers, and miners in the region.

Cashup spared no expense in building his dream. The hotel measured 66 feet by 66 feet, with a massive ballroom on the main level surrounded by a balcony where patrons could watch the goings-on below. Guests entered the hotel through an ornate parlor, whose walls were "festooned with garlands of lush grains that grew so well in the fertile surroundings," according to amateur historian Randall Johnson. The ballroom's stage often featured the Privett Brothers Orchestra, Cashup's favorite musicians. Cashup often got on stage to join brothers Cy and Andy Privett, who came fifteen miles north from Colfax to play the minuet, the polka, the quadrille, and the waltz. Music filled the hotel late into the night and, yes, into daylight, when others were already up and being productive.

On the very top of the hotel sat a 14-foot by 14-foot cupola that opened to the skies, a vista that resembled one offered by an ocean steamer deck. "From this exalted standpoint, aided by the powerful glass, a wonderland is exposed to view," reported the Spokesman-Review after the grand opening. Patrons felt like they were on the bridge of a ship sailing across the Palouse, "affording a vision of 150 miles over the now productive hills unfolding as rolling pillows in every direction." The actual distance one could see from up there depended not just on how clear the skies were but also on how much exaggeration the newspaper writer was willing to infuse. Fifty miles? One hundred? One hundred fifty?

Perhaps the most fantastical gimmick conjured up by Cashup was what could only be considered advanced high tech at the time. Local newspapers called it the "magic lantern" show: "A contrivance by which [guests] could look through a hole in the wall at pictures which were seen through magnifying lenses and under powerful lights and were really beautiful." The result, with perhaps some smoke added, was that the images appeared to be moving—a year before Edison invented the motion picture back east.

The magic lantern shows, the orchestras, the stage, operatic singers, Punch and Judy shows: Cashup's hotel offered entertainment not found in many other grand hotels. In fact, references to magic lantern shows occurring in the western United States during this era are rare in the historical record. The elaborate and much bigger San Francisco Palace Hotel, built from California gold rush money, didn't host the shows; nor did Spokane's finest hotels, the Western and the Californian. Smaller hotels in Colfax and Walla Walla offered little more than a place to sleep and maybe get a meal. Cashup's hotel was a game changer.

Indeed, what Cashup had built—an elaborate entertainment hotel in the middle of nowhere—was not unlike what Thomas Hull did in 1941 with the El Rancho Vegas Hotel, the first hotel on what would become the Las Vegas Strip.

The *Spokane Review* (later renamed *Spokesman-Review*) called it a "great northwestern pleasure resort." The hotel was the talk of the territory. "Cashup had a mania for company, and the bigger the crowd and the longer it stayed the better his mood," wrote the newspaper in 1919. "Each swain and every belle came at dusk, prepared to dance until daylight. On occasion the merrymakers would find themselves snowed in, and would stay for days, or until the weather broke."

It had been unlike any place around. Groundbreaking. And now, in 1911, it was on fire.

To see the building going up in flames hurt Ferd deep inside his heart. After his father died fifteen years prior, his brother J. F. Davis tried to run the hotel. That added three more years. But its slow death continued until J. F. boarded it up and moved off the butte for good.

Even after it closed, the family felt that the hotel belonged to them. Thus the finality of the fire was excruciating. It was painful to see the flames destroying their father's legendary hotel, a roaring orange flickering in the night sky that was visible to all onlookers within a hundred-mile radius.

Josephine Jodel Bye, a twenty-four-year-old farmer's wife, could see the flames from the front porch of her family home in tiny Princeton, Idaho, nearly thirty miles east. Josephine and her family had moved to the region two years prior to manage a dairy farm at the nearby Potlatch Lumber Mill. But that night, as her granddaughter Donna Gwinn remembers Josephine's story, "she saw this great big plume of smoke to the west. 'Oh! That might be the hotel!' She used an expression in her voice that makes me remember her experience."

Just a few miles away from the Byes, the daughter of rancher J. E. Tate saw the flames that night, too. "I lived on a ranch near Fallon [Washington, twenty miles southeast of Steptoe Butte]" she wrote in a 1969 letter. "We had talked about going up to Steptoe Butte to see Cashup Davis's place and staying all night. We could see it plainly from our farm," she said. "In those days the travel was by horse and buggy. We would have stayed all night as it was too long of a trip for the team . . . My father—J. E. Tate—came and informed us that the Hotel was burning. We all rushed out and looked—and it was a great sight."

It was the biggest show ever seen by Cashup's expansive circle of friends, admirers, and former guests throughout the region. The fire lit the countryside. Many said it resembled a volcano. The *Tekoa Sentinel* wrote that "the fiery spectacle was viewed in silence by the townspeople of Oakesdale."

The telescope that Ferd used to watch the flames once stood in the cupola at the hotel's pinnacle, where guests elbowed each other for the chance to look through it, "through which guests could see all the way to Walla Walla," one hundred miles to the southwest, "and beyond," reported the *Spokane Review* in 1892. The experience was likely the first time looking through a telescope for many of the hotel guests. "A telescope second in power to only one other in Washington," gushed the *Review*. Much like Cashup wanted for everything related to the historic structure, the telescope was a feature as grand as the hotel, allowing guests the stellar vision Cashup embraced. It was tragic irony that that very same telescope afforded onlookers a view of the hotel as it perished.

From the *Tekoa Sentinel*: "The building on the topmost crest of this huge mass of earth . . . no longer stands out as the attraction to recall to the minds of the Palouse pioneers times of excitement, when the Palouse was yet in infancy."

"Many a friend and acquaintance of Cashup Davis shed tears of regret as they witnessed, from afar, the obliteration of the structure which had marked but another shattered dream of fortune," wrote Karl P. Allen, a newspaperman at the *Pullman Herald* who had spent memorable evenings in the hotel and had befriended Cashup. Cashup was shrewd enough to make sure the newspaperman always had fun at his grand hotel.

The hotel was gone. The family lives on.

I owned the telescope for many years. In the 1990s, my father Aubrey, Cashup's grandson, passed it down to me. When I first laid my hands on the historic family telescope, I could feel

Cashup's presence. It was a dramatic turning point in my journey to understand Cashup, to get to know my mentor, my inspiration, even though I had never met him.

In 2020, I gave the telescope to the Whitman County Historical Society to put on permanent display, and it often travels to local libraries across the Palouse. To me, the telescope symbolizes Cashup's vision. It has the ultimate double meaning: Cashup's vision literally symbolized by an instrument of vision. Ferd completed the circle by using the telescope to watch the hotel burn. The telescope remains a symbol of an iconic man, ahead of his time, who refused to limit his visionary ambitions.

Cashup is timeless. And so are the lessons learned from his extraordinary life. His real story—his fate, the foundation of his "never say never" character, the construction of who he became— all started as a young man when he saw something peering down at him. What he saw up there would manifest itself later in his life in a way he could have never imagined.

TWO

CASTLES IN THE AIR

"If you don't build castles in the air, you won't build anything on the ground."

VICTOR HUGO

I HAVE OFTEN THOUGHT ABOUT my great-grandfather when he was in his twenties. When I do, I cannot help but be reminded of my life when I left my parents' dairy farm in Deer Park, a charming farm town a few miles north of the Palouse, to go to college at Washington State University. I was fired up, loaded with ambition.

To more fully understand James "Cashup" Davis, you need to know that he was an overachiever from early on in his life. Confident and competent, short in stature but outgoing with a big personality, he possessed great enthusiasm for life and for anything in life. He could convince just about anyone of just about anything. Numerous historical accounts indicate that when James put his mind to something, he pursued it relentlessly. He had all the tools for building an extraordinary life.

Something loomed over young James Davis as he grew up. Born in England in 1815, he lived in Hastings until he left for America in 1841. Part of the British environment likely caught his fascination and admiration, sparking the ambition of a motivated young man and shaping the way he embraced big ideas and their grand expression. Castles abound in southern England, towering over the tops of its green hills and craggy cliffs. Given their prevalence throughout Britain, the castles' majestic appearance likely influenced how James envisioned his life and work in America.

Only many years later, after crossing an ocean and a continent, would James earn the nickname "Cashup" in the rough-and-tumble American West, where he ultimately committed his life to chasing the grand vision of a hotel building atop a massive butte: a romantic notion, a fantasy, one that eventually became a real castle touching the sky over Steptoe Butte.

Inspiring castles dotted the cliffs in southeast England where he was born and where he spent most of his life before going to America. The names of the castles are etched into the minds of the people in the region: Bodiam. Arundel. Herstmonceux. Hever. Dover. They were built on the cliffs, standing guard over the English countryside. It is easy to be captivated by their grandeur, strength, nobility, and splendor. Perhaps James admired the role castles played in providing safety and protection for townspeople from all manner of threats. He may have seen that castles were the center of attention for politics and culture during turbulent times—places where communities gathered to talk, dance, and celebrate.

Whatever fascination James may have had with castles, they were a near constant presence for him during three distinct facets of his life in Britain: growing up, touring the United Kingdom with a military captain, and helping to build the Dover Tunnel.

James was born on November 16, 1815, the first of nine children born to his father, William, a red-headed stone mason and carpenter, and his mother, twenty-four-year-old Frances "Fanny" Smith Davis. According to family notes, Fanny was "tiny with curly, black hair" and was "a sparkling woman." The family lived just west of Hastings in East Sussex County. James's birth was only a few months before Britain's Duke of Wellington defeated Napoleon at Waterloo. The victory ushered in decades of relative peace for England.

Hastings is where William the Conqueror first set foot on British soil to begin the Norman Conquest, nearly 750 years before James's birth. William built many castles throughout England, beginning with one right there in Hastings. Indeed, one of James's younger brothers, Trayton, "played in the shadow of Battle Abbey," which had been built by William to commemorate his Hastings victory. As a boy, James watched as the ruined Hastings Castle, perched on a bluff on the edge of the sea in the heart of the old town, was excavated and returned to a degree of glory that brought visitors from throughout England. It was a source of pride for the residents of Hastings.

When he was eleven, James and his family lived on an estate owned by Lord Trayton (the nobleman after whom his brother was named). The estate, where the town of St. Leonards-on-Sea would eventually be built, provided lots of work for James's father and the boys.

Other castles were nearby: ten miles to the west, ten miles to the north, and ten miles to the east. To the north was Bodiam Castle, a fortress built in 1385, rising from the center of a massive moat and widely considered to be one of the most attractive castles in Britain. To the west were the noble ruins of Herstmonceux Castle, which had stood since the fifteenth century. And to the east: the Ypres Tower, built in 1249, still standing as part of the fortifications for two towns, Rye and Winchelsea, which helped the settlements fend off seafaring invasions. These castles were designed to impress, to endure the ravages of time, and to bring people together—purposes that seemed to surface later in James's life in America.

James learned lessons from his enterprising father William, who "dealt in timber for shipbuilding purposes—built turnpike gates—dug wells . . . The Napoleonic Wars had brought great demand for new ships, and many were built at Hastings." But William died relatively young, when James was likely in his teens or early twenties. "At the age of 50, or thereabouts," says the family history, "he was killed in a well he was digging." Few other details exist.

Hastings, with its history of dramatic ups and downs, soon appealed to Britons who had the time and income to go on vacation at a desirable seaside resort. Its population ballooned to more than 10,000 residents by 1830. In that same year, James, at fifteen years old, left the "common schools" (the name given to schools with a higher reputation) to live with Col. William Short, a paternal uncle. James was given responsibilities early on, entering the Royal Family Riding School in order to be put in charge of driving a pair of Shetland ponies, a gift to Lord and Lady Erskine from Mahmud II, the sultan of the Ottoman Empire (later Turkey). Lord Erskine's family had a rich, diplomatic history in America and although there is no evidence to suggest that the young man tending the ponies interacted extensively with the Erskine clan, it may have been James's first direct hint at life in America, the land of freedom and enterprise.

James's brush with aristocracy also led to an introduction to Capt. John Gwynn. Very little has been written about the captain and the spelling of his last name has several variations. But he travelled extensively throughout the United Kingdom—Ireland, Scotland, Wales—bringing young James along with him as an aide. In such a role, James would have been surrounded by respectful conduct, high culture, worldly insights, self-discipline, and examples of leadership. When Captain Gwynn died in Brighton just a year and a half after James became his aide, James found a window of time to travel through France and visit other parts of Europe on his own. His desire to see places beyond England surely increased.

By 1830, the world's first steam locomotive lines were hauling passengers in Britain. It was a confident time for the nation, full of momentum in industry and social change; yet many were still fighting off hardships. In 1838, work began on what is arguably the most well-known and most difficult train tunnel in all of England: the Dover Tunnel under Shakespeare Cliff. James, now in his early twenties, went to work on the tunnel as an employee of the McIntosh and Bowland company. Honing his leadership skills, he led a team of sixty men who had to snake the tunnel and rail lines through treacherous cliffs, moving mountains of rock. The project was not universally embraced, however. Opponents, quoting Shakespeare's play King Lear, argued that the work would deface the famous Dover chalk cliffs, so popular with early postcards. In his thesis "Early British Railway Tunnels," University of York professor Hubert Pragnell writes that leading citizens assured "admirers of our great bard (poet)" that the cliff which bore Shakespeare's name still "rears its 330-foot head undisfigured, and, as they would say, undesecrated [sic]." Pragnell writes, "Even before the line opened it received the acclamation of newspapers, travel journals and guidebooks alike. The bore of Shakespeare Cliff Tunnel was completed as early as November 1839 'with its lofty Gothic arches beginning to shadow forth its ultimate effect.'" The Duke of Wellington even paid an unexpected visit to Dover, where, as Pragnell writes, he walked "the entire length of the Shakespeare Cliff Tunnel and the Duke expressed himself 'highly delighted at the construction of the tunnel . . . a marvelous piece of engineering and a lasting testimony to man's ingenuity in almost impossible conditions.'"

James had valuable attributes—youth, success, a strong work ethic, leadership skills—and big thinking. He did not know it yet, but he could surely build a grand hotel in a most difficult location. At the age of twenty-five, James could no longer resist the greatest

Vintage postcard with an image of the Shakespeare Cliff Dover Tunnel, which James Davis, as a young man, helped to construct. Detroit Publishing Company, 1905. Downloaded from Wikimedia Commons.

adventure of all: America. Europeans were leaving for America by the hundreds of thousands every year at that point. And James was among them—not fleeing from hunger or tyranny, but by choice. He wanted to live the American concept. He wanted to be an American. His uncle, Miller Davis, had sailed to America previously and had settled in Ohio, where he built a home and "lived in luxurious style," as the uncle conveyed to the family back in England, with the same kind of enthusiasm for life that James would later demonstrate.

On August 8, 1841, James and his brother Sivyer traveled a few miles eastward up the coast to the Port of Deal, where, according to Lloyd's passenger manifest, they boarded the packet ship *Quebec*, which had departed from London on the prior leg. The ship had a cargo of chalk from the cliffs the two brothers knew well, which likely was a key reason it had stopped at the port. The next day, as the ship left the dock and headed southward to

An excerpt from the passenger manifest for the packet ship *Quebec* in August 1841. James and Sivyer Davis are listed on lines 5 and 6. From Passenger Lists of Vessels Arriving at New York, New York, 1820-1897. Microfilm Publication M237, 675 rolls. NAI: 6256867. Records of the US Customs Service, Record Group 36. National Archives at Washington, DC, via Ancestry.com and Sharon Hall, researcher.

round the southern tip of England, the Deal Castle loomed in the distance—a grand tower consisting of a succession of turrets: a main, large round turret perched upon six turrets that, in turn, perch upon six more. The view provided one final imprint of the grand castles of England as James made his way to the western unknown.

While most European immigrants of the day brought tools with them to improve their work options upon arrival, and perhaps some clothes and a family bible, James brought so much more, a testament to his early success in life: "A team of driving horses, a surrey [a four-wheeled doorless carriage], his rifle and a pair of hounds." And his most prized possession—an ornate service sword bequeathed to him by his uncle, Colonel Short, upon his death.

With all this in hand, they set off for America, the beginning of a new chapter of Cashup Davis's extraordinary life that would take him to unexpected places and have him do unexpected things—an American way of living that would have been hard for many British citizens of that time to conjure. Indeed, if anyone had told James then what he was going to encounter in the years ahead, even he might not have believed the story.

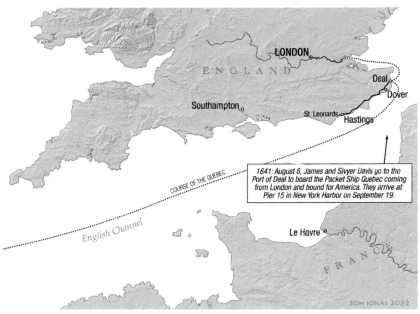

1841: August 8, James and Sivyer Davis go to the Port of Deal to board the Packet Ship Quebec coming from London and bound for America. They arrive at Pier 15 in New York Harbor on September 19.

Route of the *Quebec* from London to Deal and points west.

THREE

ADVENTURE IN AMERICA

"My own feeling is, he decided, 'I'll know where I want to go when I get there.'"

RANDALL JOHNSON, HISTORIAN

ALMOST EVERYTHING ABOUT AMERICA WAS different.

On Sunday, September 19, 1841, James and Sivyer finished their forty-four-day Atlantic crossing and sailed into New York Harbor. The ship docked at Pier 15 at the foot of South Street, smack in the middle of a nonstop churn of unloading, delivering, and transporting, and mere yards from Wall Street. In the beautiful autumn weather that year, the sun shown on the face of every immigrant stepping off the *Quebec* that day and into an uncertain new life in America.

Even the air seemed different. It seemed filled with possibility. It was almost tangible.

Unlike any other nation, the United States of America in 1841 was a nation on a mission to get somewhere, to refine its grand experiment as the world's first true democracy. The pace of life was fast because it was up to each person to get where he or she wanted to go, without a king or a tyrant or a lineage determining the path. To be clear, life was not easy and could be cruel and brutal. But, for the most part, immigration was a self-selecting dynamic: people who chose to come to America were more likely to be eager to work hard and make something of their lives—a dynamic that America has enjoyed for many generations. And James fit right in. Yet he was different in some ways too. He already had a better life. He had relative wealth. He wanted—and got—so much more.

Opportunity was aspirational. America was very much a country steeped in problems too—problems that a nation of people had to fix:

- The American president, William Henry Harrison, had recently died after only a month in office, sending national politics into turmoil.
- Fights over slavery were raging in the courts, in Congress, in town squares, and back alleys—even though the Civil War was still two decades away. Slavery had been banned in England in 1833, so James had not seen slavery in nearly a decade. A Black man named Frederick Douglass was about to shake the American body politic in November, when he gave his first anti-slavery speech at a meeting of the Plymouth County Anti-Slavery Society.
- Mexicans and Texans and others were starting to fire at each other more and more along an uncertain southern border.
- American newspapers expressed outrage at British Canadian forces, who in 1837 had crossed into US territory to attack the American steamboat *Caroline* near Niagara Falls. It led to the Webster-Ashburton Treaty, which defined the American-Canadian border east of the Rocky Mountains.
- Native American tribes had been forcibly moved from their land after Congress passed the Indian Removal Act in 1830. The Seminoles, one of the few tribes

who successfully resisted removal, were waging war against American military men deep in the Florida Everglades in the Second Seminole War.

- Americans were even fighting—and sometimes firing at—other Americans over what constituted a true democracy, as was the case that year in the Dorr Rebellion in Providence, Rhode Island, which eventually led to overturning the state constitution's voting requirement of land ownership.
- Labor unions and strikes were bolstered by key legal cases working their way through the courts as workers fought for a better life.
- Gold had just been discovered in Placerita Canyon in Rancho San Francisco, California, although the California Gold Rush era was officially still about eight years away.

And James landed smack in the middle of all of this in 1841. Immigrants were not all welcome in 1841 America. James was more fortunate. He was British, with wealth, intellect, charisma, wit, a plan, and a hint of aristocracy—although he wasn't the kind of man to wallow in it. He was affable and maintained an unimposing physical presence. Indeed, he won over people with his charm.

If James had stayed in New York City, one can only imagine the wealth and notoriety he may have gained. Surely, he read the American headlines about the wealthiest men of the day: John Jacob Astor (a German immigrant with big plans for the Pacific Northwest), Cornelius Vanderbilt (who founded one of the steamboat lines on the Hudson that James was about to board), and John D. Rockefeller (the patriarch of the burgeoning Rockefeller oil dynasty). Even the owners of the shipping line that brought him to America—Grinnell, Minturn & Company—were billionaires two and three times over in today's equivalent dollars. But James's destiny was not New York.

On his first morning in America, the sun rose at 5:57 a.m. You can bet he was up and already starting Day One with vim and vigor. A headline that day in the *New York Tribune* perhaps captured his optimism, heralding, "The Will of a Nation, Uncontrolled by the Will of One Man," the very definition of the distinction between new America and old England. The paper was run by Horace Greeley, who is often given credit for the phrase "go west, young man" that would define James's life. The *Tribune* was filled with departure times for steamboats leaving New York's many docks and heading up the Hudson River to Albany and other points north—the route James and Sivyer were about to take. There was bustle. The Troy Steamboat Line was leaving from the foot of Cortlandt Street. Vanderbilt's The People's Line departed from the pier at Liberty Street. The vessels were named the *Diamond*, *Cinderella*, *Highlander*, *North America*, *Water Witch*, and *DeWitt Clinton*. Freight was generally charged at fifty cents per hundred pounds, payable directly to the ship's captain. People were leaving New York and fanning out throughout the region and across America. After staying in New York for a week, James and his brother joined them.

After the Davis brothers reached Albany via the Hudson River, they continued westward to the Erie Canal, which had been open for just fifteen years. When American entrepreneurs dug that canal, connecting the Great Lakes to the Atlantic Ocean—despite predictions doubting that it was even possible—it was immediately considered an engineering marvel. James got a first-hand look during the dawn of his American experience. What must have been going through his mind?

The brothers then traveled westward across Lake Ontario and Lake Erie to a small inland town called Scipio, Ohio, founded eighteen years earlier, where white settlers had lived for only fifty years and remnants of Indian wigwams were still seen. At the time, this region was the American West; some authorities even called it "the far west." It had been James's goal to reach the American West, and, arriving in Scipio, he did. But the definition of the American West kept changing with westward expansion. James and Sivyer stayed with their uncle Miller Davis who was, indeed, living in style, "though in a house built without a nail," a notable departure from building standards in England, and one of myriad new conventions they were discovering in America.

European immigrants were rapidly populating the area in and around Scipio. German language newspapers operated in the Great Lakes region. But a British presence was even clearer. Villages near Scipio, like New London, adopted town names familiar to those across the Atlantic Ocean. Taverns and mills, clothiers, and churches housing religions familiar to Brits were everywhere, as were British surnames. There were a plethora of Davises, even a Davis cemetery nearby, which was later moved so the dirt could be turned to raise crops.

For a man intending to go to the American West in 1841, Scipio, Ohio, was thus it. For the next year or two, James earned a good living in his trade as a stone mason because of his experience building the Dover Tunnel. Scipio was a busy little town: William D. Jones, a Welshman, owned the first tavern in the village, a two-story log-house. John Hydee ran the sawmill, although new ones were opening up all over. Reuben George and John A. Applegate ran the post office, which moved around quite a bit. This was James's first real taste of America.

Just two years after James and Sivyer arrived in America, their mother Frances—a widow now for many years—and their brothers and sisters followed them to Ohio. They quickly made something of themselves using their skills from England. Digging wells made them some money and notoriety; "there was a serious water shortage, and a local history records that 'Thanks to

Messrs. Davis of England, three public wells were dug to a depth of 65 feet.'"

Frances found America unusual, according to an unsigned handwritten compilation of family notes. One story about James's mother in particular became a family favorite: "When they first came, a neighbor told her to help themselves to all the green field corn they wanted. She had never seen corn. So she went into the field, looked it over and the only thing she could see that she considered edible was the silks. So she gathered a panful and took it home and boiled it! The family decided that, if that was American corn, they did not like it."

Thus began James's American whirlwind journey. He did not realize then that he would eventually settle in a place many had never heard of, but James's circuitous path to the Palouse region was underway.

After a couple of years with his uncle, James moved to Franklin County, Ohio, along the Scioto River near Columbus, which had been founded twenty-eight years before his arrival. He was likely to have seen some of the Indian mounds that dotted the region: burial grounds from several tribes, including the Adena and Hopewell. Indian battles, having been waged for nearly one hundred years already, continued into the middle 1800s. As the city of Columbus grew, the clay from some of the sacred Indian mounds was used for bricks to build the earliest towers in the city and the statehouse.

James met and began courting an impressive American woman named Mary Ann Shoemaker and on September 4, 1844, they married. (As sources vary as to how she was commonly called, we refer to her throughout this work as "Mary Ann.") She was seventeen years old and he was twenty-nine. Just three years after arriving in America, James now had an American wife from a highly respected family. Family notes said Mary Ann had been living in "Columbia, Ohio" (more likely they meant Columbus) and was originally from a very prominent Pennsylvania family that had arrived in America in the 1600s. Her family lineage may have played a role in some crucial life decisions that we will explore later. Little did Mary Ann know that she was about to begin a life of adventure and a near constant search for something else, something better, something bigger in an America where anything seemed possible.

As James's great-grandson, I cannot help but believe an "anything-seems-possible" mentality made up the core of his view of life. His "pursuit of excellence," even at this young age, would guide him and become a gift he would leave to his descendants and to anyone else. Yet he was many years away from knowing more. Perhaps he never would know it.

After they were married, James and Mary Ann lived in Sandusky, Ohio, on the shores of Lake Erie, where they had their first child, William, in August 1846. Slowly but surely, they moved farther and farther west.

Just after William's birth, James and Mary Ann packed up the baby and all their belongings and moved from Ohio to Beaver Dam, Wisconsin, about fifteen miles west of LeRoy, fifty miles from the shores of Lake Michigan. They likely traveled part of the distance from Ohio on a steamboat, an extremely popular mode of transportation on the lakes. Not long after that, they moved more than one hundred miles farther inland and west to the La Crosse River Valley, near a fledgling town called Sparta, Wisconsin. James and Mary Ann were now ahead of the general westward expansion, preceding by a year or two the first white settlers whose land claims founded Sparta, according to the town's own written history. Military roads had been built into this wilderness. The Winnebago, Sauk, and Fox tribes tried to keep white settlement out but were unsuccessful. Scuffles occurred. Some violence too. Eventually, the indigenous peoples were coerced into signing treaties that ceded their land claims. Later, the American military forcibly removed

The James Davis family in Wisconsin, circa 1864. This is the earliest known photo of James Davis. Having arrived in America twenty-three years earlier, he is married and has ten children (the eleventh is born in 1867). From the collection of Jim Martin.

remaining Native American tribes who refused to recognize the treaties. Even those remaining Native Americans who had been removed trickled back over time to the region around Sparta and continued living on the land as they had for thousands of years.

James and Mary Ann acquired land and farmed and thus had early experience in how to live in relative harmony with Native Americans, even though white settlers were taking the latter's land and chipping away at their way of life. If the roads and the increased white settlement weren't enough to threaten the tribes, trains came into the region and the gush of arriving white people increased exponentially.

Amid all this change in Wisconsin, James and Mary Ann expanded their family to eleven children: seven boys and four girls: William A., born April 20, 1846; Laura C., June 20, 1848; Frances L., February 25, 1850; Ferdinand A., June 4, 1852; Henry E., July 30, 1853; James P., September 23, 1855; John, October 15, 1857; Clarence C., November 27, 1859; Mary Ann, February 14,

1862; Amy C., June 16, 1864; and Charles J., January 3, 1867, who eventually became my grandfather. Unlike so many families of the era, no child of the Davis family was lost to infant death. Remarkably, all his children lived well into adulthood.

I think about my own family growing up on the dairy farm. We had five in the family. Later, my wife and I had four members in our family. And it is work! James and Mary Ann bore eleven children, as many other families did in 1800s America. I cannot imagine the effort and wherewithal required to manage such a large family. On the horizon was much more work and relocation and all the danger and adventure it would bring for the thirteen-member Davis family.

Gradually, James's mother and most of his brothers and sisters also moved farther west to Wisconsin and some eventually to Kansas. Frances, once in Wisconsin, remarried in 1861 at the age of seventy-one to a man from her own Sussex County in England, William Harmer, who had been widowed. She moved onto his farm in Springvale, in Fond du Lac County, Wisconsin.

While James and Mary Ann were establishing their family, nearly every newspaper in America was headlining the California Gold Rush of 1848. James did not take the bait. Rather than dash away from his family, he stayed put in Wisconsin and continued to care for them. His family would turn out to play a crucial role in his life, which arguably never became clear to him but will become to us as this book unfolds.

Even while hunkered down in remote farmland of western Wisconsin, James could not avoid the escalating fight over slavery that divided citizens of the United States. When America plunged into civil war, James stepped up on September 17, 1861, to defend the country that had already given him so much opportunity. He had been in America for twenty years and was ready to put his life on the line for his adopted country and for the right of all people to be free. Military records show a James Davis from Monroe County

An original tin-type image of James Davis, 1866. From the collection of John Rupp and Linda Banken, descendants of Mary Ann Davis.

enlisted as a private: "Enlisted in the Wisconsin 5th Light Artillery Battery on 17 Sept 1861. Mustered out on 06 Jun 1865 at Madison, WI," two months after the official end of the war. Whether James remained in Wisconsin during the war years or whether he was shipped out closer to the front lines remains unclear. With a wife and eight children at that time, the oldest only in his teens, it would have been disastrous had James been injured in war, or worse.

For twenty-two years, the family prospered in Sparta. For most families, that would put an end to drastic changes or relocations. Not James. He was restless, still.

Iowa was next. It is unclear what drew James and Mary Ann to Iowa. But in 1866, a few years after the end of the Civil War, they pulled up stakes, sold their land, packed up their family and belongings, and moved 150 miles to the southwest, to Sumner in Bremer County, Iowa. Farming remained his mainstay there as well.

His mother, still in Wisconsin, passed away on July 17, 1868. She was buried "in a little rural cemetery Hamlet of Rogersville, Fond du Lac County, Wisconsin about 10 miles north of Waupum," wrote Julia Davis Eckhart in her family history. Rogersville is an unincorporated community adjacent to the town of Lamartine, Wisconsin. Frances's grave and that of her second husband, William, are located in the tiny and tidy Rogersville Cemetery. Theirs was an immigrant story: the couple, both from Essex County, England, and both widowed, met in the American Midwest, fell in love late in life, married, and now forever rest in America, their adopted homeland.

James had long been without his father's guidance. Now he was without his mother as well. As the eldest child, he had long been the leader of the family. Yes, he had a wonderful wife and a cadre of children. Yet—as for anyone who has lost both parents—it was a new phase in his life.

Mary Ann Davis, Cashup's Best Friend

John Rupp, a great-great-grandson of James and Mary Ann, arrives at a family storage unit in Kennewick after driving across the state of Washington. It is fall 2020. For an hour or more, he rummages through dusty boxes, files, and trunks, looking for the original letter written by Mary Ann on January 18, 1870—the earliest known family letter and one of only a handful conveying words directly from Mary Ann or James.

Frustrated, Rupp cannot find the letter. Undaunted, he travels to his sister's home in Redmond, Washington, to search through more boxes, files, and trunks. His sister, Linda Banken, also a great-great-grandchild of James and Mary Ann, is as ferocious as John in researching and documenting the Cashup Davis story.

Linda's large dining room table is not large enough for their stockpile of family history. She proudly pulls out an original 12- by 24-inch charcoal sketch of Mary Ann done from a photograph. The photographer must have sat with Mary Ann in the 1860s, before she came out to the Palouse. In the black-and-white sketch, her eye color is impossible to confirm, but they appear light-colored and as piercing as any eyes you have ever seen. Strong and no-nonsense, yet thoughtful and full of personality, they seem to be saying, "I don't want to be sitting here in all this fuss, but I do without hesitation what must be done." She wears an ornate, white, raised collar—inspired perhaps by the Victorian ruff collars of England—wrapped in dark ribbon that cascades down onto a dark dress with broad shoulders, almost like the robe of a judge. Her hair is parted in the middle, pulled back severely, and tied behind her head. But she styled her bangs to drape over the rest of her pulled-back hair, suggesting her as a woman who either cares about how she looks or one who acquiesces to a photographer's directions. She tilts her head ever so slightly to the side.

The structure of her face, however, is what is so remarkable. Her features create the Davis face that is strikingly obvious even 150 years later in numerous descendants. Her face in the sketch is strong, chiseled, broad. Combined with James's prominent bones and deep-set eyes, the Davis face is unmistakable, even on John and Linda, while they continue looking for Mary Ann's original

A sketch of Mary Ann (Shoemaker) Davis, done from a photograph (now lost). Artist unknown. From the collection of John Rupp and Linda Banken, descendants of Mary Ann Davis. Restored by Jim Martin.

letter that they know must be here somewhere, quietly fearing the remote possibility of its disappearance.

Tucked away in a plastic folder inside a thick book marked with a yellow sticky note, they find the letter. John and Linda carefully pull it out from its protective cover. It is folded and

Mary Ann's 1870 letter to her son Will, in which she notes the "Oregon Fever" gripping many in the region. From the collection of John Rupp and Linda Banken, descendants of Mary Ann Davis.

delicate—someone decades ago repaired it with cellophane tape. Someone in another generation scribbled on it, laying claim to it.

One piece of paper, folded into four pages. Written with a fountain pen in the script of the era, with the date, January 18, 1870.

Some of her letter, with spelling errors fixed by the author in this instance, describes life in Iowa and what lies ahead:

"Jim was pretty sick. I stopped at Western Union and got some conditioning powders for him. He was sick about two weeks.

"There was a ball at Cass Hall. They have one every month . . . There were 75 couples . . . two dollars a couple. That was the last ball. They are having lively times.

"We butchered yesterday 7 hogs and old Bets she was pretty fat. Pork is 6 cents a pound, wheat 35 cents, oats 25 cents a bushel. Pretty good to pay up debts."

And then, as if just another paragraph in a meandering family letter, Mary Ann drops this bombshell: "We sold Charley [a horse] for $175. We have all the rest of the horses yet your father has got the Oregon fever. He says he is going to start in two weeks if he can raise the money."

Oregon Fever? The big move west is brewing—indeed, imminent. "They give a flattering account of the country," she says, without a hint of dissent. John Rupp holds the letter tenderly and says, "I think, of all the items we've got from the Davis family, this is probably the most special item." They smile at each other, proud to be descendants of Mary Ann and James.

Mary Ann's letter says James is selling off assets to bring in funding for the family's arduous and most uncertain move yet: to the farthest reaches of the western United States, where they assume dirt has never been turned before. A person could claim 320 acres for himself or 640 acres for a married couple and work the land as they see fit. By the date of this letter, several of their eleven children are young adults. The eldest three will not embark on this journey: William Ambrose at age 24, Laura at 22, and Frances, 20. They already had lives they were developing and enjoying in the Midwest.

James and Mary Ann did, indeed, head west from Iowa in late summer 1870, with their younger children: Ferd, 19; Henry, 18; Jim P., 15; John, 13; Clarence, 11; Mary Ann, 8; Amy Charlotte, 6 (the great-grandmother of John Rupp and Linda Banken); and Charley (my grandfather), just 3 years old.

But imagine—just imagine!—bringing six boys and two girls, ranging from nineteen to three years old, across the Wild West of America in 1870!

One of the biggest unanswered questions was how James got all of them to Oregon. It has been a befuddling mystery. Here are several possible scenarios.

Wagon Train

Did the Davis family head west by wagon train, as many have believed for years? At the time, the family lived east of Omaha. Pioneers heading from Omaha to Oregon took from three and a half months up to six months to make the trip. Riding a horse could get you about forty miles a day and a lot of soreness. Hiring a professional stagecoach using six horses would get you seventy to one hundred miles a day, costing about 10 cents a mile. Wildlife along the routes at this time was already somewhat depleted, according to the writings of some pioneers, and no longer easy to find. All provisions had to be hauled. A family would commonly carry possessions like guns and knives, tools to start a new life, wooden barrels and sacks of grain, a butter churn, a kettle, cooking and storage vessels, a hand plow, and clothing. Many families could not resist bringing a trunk full of family treasures and heirlooms. James brought his prized sword from England.

Covered wagons or "prairie schooners" could carry 10,000 pounds of freight using 10, 20, even 30 oxen, horses, or mules. Local Indians would occasionally give these overland caravans a real scare for invading their land. Most pioneers formed wagon trains comprised of multiple families, often formed from prior acquaintance or those that merged during the trek.

But the wagon train theory has many problems. Chief among them is timing. The family was listed in the August 1870 census as living in Iowa. The written record puts James in Oregon in February 1871. It is very unlikely that James would have risked his family's safety by having them travel for five months in a covered wagon during autumn and winter.

Around Cape Horn

Sailing around the southern tip of South America began in earnest in 1849 for many pioneers and Gold Rush speculators. It took about six months to get from the East Coast of the United States to California by sailing south. And it was by no means safe. The Davis family could have saved time by sailing down the Mississippi River from Iowa and departing from the Gulf of Mexico. The trip could be shortened even more by their disembarking at Panama, hauling themselves and their possessions across the isthmus, then boarding a second ship headed north to San Francisco. Quite an ordeal for a large family that included very young children.

Sailing around the horn was mentioned in a 1960 Oregon newspaper obituary about James and Mary Ann's youngest daughter, Amy Charlotte (the family pronounces it "shar-LOT-ee"), who lived the longest of the Davis children. In 1957, when she was ninety-four years old, Amy Charlotte wrote, "Just think, I'm the only one out of my folk that is alive to tell the story—lone sheep without a herder." The Oregon obituary provides more details about her and the trip, though some of it is questionable. Its claim that "at the age of seven [Amy Charlotte] sailed with her parents on the 'Orephleni' [sic] from New York around Cape Horn and came by covered wagon to McMinnville, Oregon in 1870" ignores the fact that Portland, Oregon, was just forty miles northeast of McMinnville, thus negating the need for any additional travel by "covered wagon."

The vessel referred to was probably the steamship *Oriflamme*. Indeed, newspaper coverage clearly identified the *Oriflamme* as among the most popular and highly regarded side-wheeler steamships on the Pacific Coast of that era. While the *Oriflamme* sometimes sailed to east Asia, most of its services involved travel between San Francisco and Portland precisely at the time of the

Davis family's trek. The only clear historical reference to New York was an announcement that wealthy stagecoach owner Ben Holladay bought the *Oriflamme* and was having it sailed from its shipyard in New York (where it was being overhauled as a Civil War fighting vessel) to Oregon for its initial delivery as a passenger vessel. If the Davis clan had sailed from New York, as the obituary claims, they would have had to travel from Iowa to New York and then around the Horn. That seems to be the long way around.

Transcontinental Railroad

The theory that makes the most sense is that James put himself and his family on the new transcontinental railroad that opened in August 1869, which connected Council Bluffs, Iowa, to the Pacific Coast. Surely, the railroad was the biggest news in Iowa for some time, beckoning to those with "Oregon fever." The easternmost terminus in Iowa hauled passengers from sister city Omaha to San Francisco in eleven "tedious jolting and bumping" days and nights, according to Palouse pioneer J. P. T. McCroskey's account to the *Pullman Herald*. According to McCroskey, the fare from Omaha to San Francisco was $65 for a third-class sleeping car—half the price of a stagecoach. The route took passengers to San Francisco, where for another $25, travelers secured steamship passage to Oregon. Going west by train also avoided encounters with Native American warriors. And, for a big family that included young children, going by train avoided prairie travel, food shortages, sickness, injury, and other threats. Completing that final leg from San Francisco to Oregon was the easy part, as it turns out. The *Oriflamme* became one of the most popular steamships for transporting passengers from San Francisco to Portland, serving thousands of travelers who had gotten off the new transcontinental railroad.

Sketch of the steamship *Oriflamme*, which ran from San Francisco to Portland, circa 1860. Image from Wright, E.W., ed. (1895) *Lewis & Dryden's Marine History of the Pacific Northwest*. Portland Oregon: The Lewis & Dryden Printing Company, p. 152. Downloaded from Wikimedia Commons.

Newspapers like the *Oregon Republican* were constantly reporting in their briefs about ships and trains, particularly the *Oriflamme*. One account noted that "several immigrant families came up by the *Oriflamme*" or "the imported stock of Mr. S. G. Reed arrived per steamer *Oriflamme* Tuesday." In fact, on a Monday in April 1871, an Oregon newspaper article proclaimed the *Oriflamme* set a speed record for the route "in fifty nine hours, said to [be] the fastest trip on reccrd [sic]."

The *Oriflamme* was also popular with VIPs. In 1871, Oregon's Gov. George Lemuel Woods left the state to become governor of the Utah territory. To begin his new job, he sailed on the *Oriflamme* from Portland to San Francisco; to reach Utah's capital in Salt Lake City, the new railroad offered a convenient ride. If that route was good enough for Governor Woods, it's not unreasonable to think that it rated the same for James Davis and his family.

One more clue. A 1924 obituary of Ferd Davis reported that he "came west by the southern route to California in the early 70s. Moving northward by boat," additional confirmation that the family likely all rode the train westward and then took the steamer north to Oregon.

Just a few months after arriving in Oregon, James made reference to the railroad route in a February 20, 1871, letter, inviting his son William to join him. He stated that "they have lowered the fare on the railroad from Omaha to fifty dollars" and then reminded his son that the cost to steam from San Francisco to Portland was just $20. Clearly, he was keenly aware of the transcontinental railroad and its more amenable cost.

The final evidence supporting the theory that James brought his family from Iowa by train and then steamer from San Francisco comes from a *Pullman Herald* article written forty years after James arrived on the Palouse by newspaperman Karl Allen. He wrote that James came "from the east and up from San Francisco 40 years ago," making no reference whatsoever to a daunting ocean voyage around the horn.

Further, S. C. Roberts, a professor from Washington State College (now Washington State University), who had known the Davis family since 1883, cited James's daughter Mary Ann when he wrote that the family "came by way of San Francisco and Portland to McMinnville, Ore." It is important to note that Roberts knew James and his family personally, visited them often, and wrote extensively about them in the 1936 newspaper series called "Pioneers I Have Known," relying on James's daughter Mary Ann as his key source. Thus Roberts is the most accurate and important chronicler of the James Davis story during the very early years.

Given the preponderance of the historical record, the Davis family likely rode from Iowa to San Francisco on the new transcontinental railroad, then took the steamer *Oriflamme* to Portland or Astoria.

The misinformation about travelling west by covered wagon came from Julia, James's granddaughter, who wrote the family history based on conversations with her father Ed and other family members as well as on newspaper articles of the time. She wrote: "They came all the way by covered wagon and horses. The younger children rode while the older members of the family walked most of the way. Sometimes they rode, but not very often." But those stories of covered wagons likely refer to the relatively short trek from Oregon to the Palouse, which was undoubtedly done via covered wagon. Notably, there are no accounts of the adventures that would have been a part of a covered wagon trek across Indian country, which would have incurred greater risk, enormous hardships, and many more months to complete.

Regardless of How You Got There, The Boom Was On

Documents and newspapers of the 1870s make it clear that an exodus to Oregon was underway in America—whether by way of the Oregon Trail or steamships or the new transcontinental railroad. Pioneers, miners, farmers, businessmen, and others were constantly arriving in Oregon towns. Salmon canneries dotted the shoreline and America suddenly fell in love with the taste of salmon. Timber, once viewed as a nuisance during white settlement, because it had to be cleared for farming and ranching, became the building material of choice.

After James and his family arrived in Oregon in 1870, they travelled thirty-five miles south of Portland to rented farmland near what is now McMinnville and its rich Yamhill Valley dirt and got to work. The area is spectacularly beautiful country and not far from the Pacific Ocean, with sloping hills, lots of trees, meandering rivers, and lush green everywhere you turn. Yamhill is now part of the exceedingly valuable Oregon wine country.

After spending a lot of money to get his family out west, it is likely that James suddenly needed more of it. In a February 20, 1871, letter, James somewhat frantically asked his son William, "I want you to try and get me some money somehow." He proposed several ideas, including borrowing against a mortgage. "I can make money here, if I had a little money to start with. This is a beautiful country." James wrote this letter during what would have been the family's first winter in the Pacific Northwest. Time to prepare the fields was ticking away. "I wrote a letter to Andrew over six weeks ago wishing him and you to raise me some money, but have not heard from any of you." If he was going to rent this farmland, "I have got to pay the man $400 for the two years[.] [N]ow I have got to raise this money by the 25th day of April next in about eight weeks. Now if there is any chance to get the money out here do your best to get it. I can pay it back again in the fall if it is needed and if there is not any chance please send me the notes and mortgage perhaps I can get some money on them here." He listed several people in Iowa who still owed him money.

As this is the first time we quote Cashup in his own words, and this letter is one of only two known to survive, we present it in its totality:

McMinnville Feb. 20th 1871 Yamhill Co. Oregon

Dear Son, I write to you hoping to find you all well as it leaves us all at present. I wrote a letter to Andrew over six weeks a go wishing him and you to raise me some Money but have not heard from any of you I think you could raise that money of Wood by throwing of the Interest and a little of the principle I want you to see if you can get some money on that Mortgage perhaps you and Andrew could do some thing with Charly [scribble] Davis I will throw of three Hundred Dollars on the Mortgage I want you to try and get me some Money some how there is a Dutchman living some were near where Fanny taught School perhaps you could do some thing with [scribble] by throwing of the Interest and ten per cent besides, you find out what Ladwig intends to pay this fall perhaps McWright can buy that Mortgage of yours, I can make money here. If I had a little money to start with this is a Beautiful Country hardly any of them that have fed any of their Cattle or their hogs or Sheep or Colts or horses that run out and they are all fat enough to kill I have just rented a farm for two years there is 580 acres in the farm 140 under the plow about one hundred more Prairie which I shall brake up this season, there is two large Orchards perhaps they will bear 2000 Bushels of Apples perhaps 200 Bushels of Pears and lots of nice tame Plumbs, Currant and Lawton Blackberys and most all kinds of Fruit I get all the Fruit and fifteen hogs for my self the man finds 1 Horse team 1 Wagon 2 plows to drag ¼ of a thrashing Machine 1 Faning Mill now I have got to pay the man $400 four hundred Dollars for the two years now I have got to raise this money by the 25th day of April next in about eight weeks now If there is any chance to get the Money out their do your best to get it I can pay it back again in the fall if it is nedded and if there is not any chance please send me the notes and Mortgage perhaps I can get some money on them here tell Wright if he has got any that he can spare five hundred dollars you can let him have them notes and Mortgage for security you see the time that I have to pay the four hundred Dollars now don't delay a moment it takes 20 days to get a letter through now if I had my Money all of it I could buy about 40 Cows and here were we have not to feed but little all the year and butter from .30 to .50 cents per pound and Calfs 10 dollars each at weinding [weaning] time and hogs run to grass all the Winter, wheat is one dollar and ten cents Coin Eggs 20 to 40 cents per doz Potatoes one dollar now the breaking that I am a going to do is not like that breaking out there we break it with one pair of horse and raise a good Crop this year I think I can raise quit a crop this year our market is on the edge of this farm the Yamhill river runs a long the edge of that farm the steam boat comes here every other day here is plenty of farms to rent here aman can Plow every month in the year but July and august and so wheat the same they are from six to eight weeks a harvesting so you see a man can get in and harvest a lot of grain in one year with one team this is the best Country I ever saw both to live and make money they are plowing and sowing now when it does not rain the old Settlers do not work much here is the best Society I ever saw in any Country the most all go to Meetings pay their Preachers well the schooling is of the very best order the highest branches taught our money is Gold and silver no money less than a ten cent peace if you buy anything for a dime and give them a two shilling peace they will give you out ten cents they have lower the fare on the rail road from Omaha to fifty Dollars you can buy your ticket East Cheaper it cost from san Francisco to Portland twenty Dollars by the Steamboat. Ed is a working out for twenty four dollars a Month now he has got a good place Jim and Frank and Corp can work our farm send me word how old Crouse likes my Chain bags and Crout cutter tell him he never paid me for that Machine yet tell him I want the Money for it and ask the other old Dutchman how he likes them Potatoes he never paid me for If you do not come out here this spring you had better let me have your money that you have to spare I will pay you 12 per cent that is what they pay here don't forget duty now write as soon as you get this you and Andrew do your best for me and perhaps I can do as much for you some time give our loves to all our and McWrights Family and give my respects to my partner poor old Sam tell him if I had him here I should be all right we are all well corp is a fat as he can be I have sent you a book and two Papers our best love to you and all

James Davis

The first page of James Davis's letter to his son, written February 20, 1871, while the family was living in Oregon. From the collection of Jim Martin.

Mentioned in James's letter is his son Ed (Henry Edward Davis), who was nineteen at the time, his son Jim (James Payne Davis), sixteen, and Frank (John Franklin Davis), fourteen. Other references to names are unknown, although "Corp" could be a favorite horse.

It's unclear whether James got the money he needed to rent the farmland along the Yamhill River, but the family farmed there for twenty-two months. By late spring or summer of 1872, James began exploring the Palouse, where he did not have to rent or even buy farmland from anyone. He wanted to homestead, to be awarded his own land by the federal government.

Many arriving in Oregon kept right on going elsewhere to find their own homestead. The Columbia River became the highway to "the Upper Country," as many called it then, from Portland and Astoria, up the Columbia to The Dalles, Umatilla, and beyond. Modest gold strikes were adding to the influx, and businesses popped up to supply all these new arrivals. The US government continued building roads deep into Indian territory, much to the Indians' increasing outrage.

As settlers grabbed the land claims in western Oregon at an increasing pace, pushing westward expansion farther and farther "in search of the 'green fields just over the hill,'" land was more plentiful up the Columbia, Allen wrote. Steamships frequently hauled freight and people up the Columbia to the next rapid, where they all had to portage around the falls or rapids—at first on foot, then on wagons, and eventually on short-run trains—then back onto steamships for the next leg. When the rivers ran high, steamships could reach all the way to Priest Rapids near what is today Pasco, Washington, or even farther east to Lewiston, Idaho. But most of the time they hauled in at Umatilla, Wallula, and Walla Walla, and travelers went overland by stagecoach, wagon, horse, mule, or on foot.

In the late spring or summer of 1872, with good weather, James left his family behind at their farmland along the Yamhill River to stake a claim for land on the Palouse. He

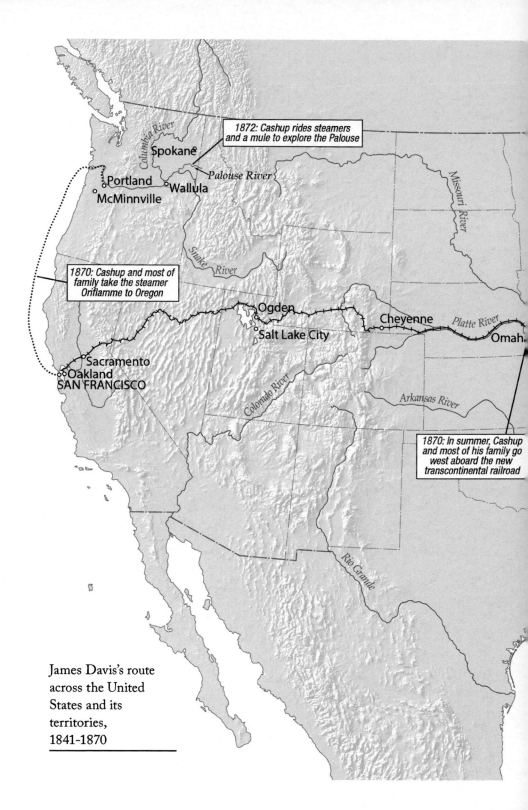

1872: Cashup rides steamers and a mule to explore the Palouse

Columbia River

Spokane

Palouse River

Portland
McMinnville
Wallula

Snake River

1870: Cashup and most of family take the steamer *Oriflamme* to Oregon

Missouri River

Ogden
Cheyenne
Platte River
Salt Lake City
Omah[a]

Sacramento
Oakland
SAN FRANCISCO

Colorado River

Arkansas River

1870: In summer, Cashup and most of his family go west aboard the new transcontinental railroad

Rio Grande

James Davis's route across the United States and its territories, 1841-1870

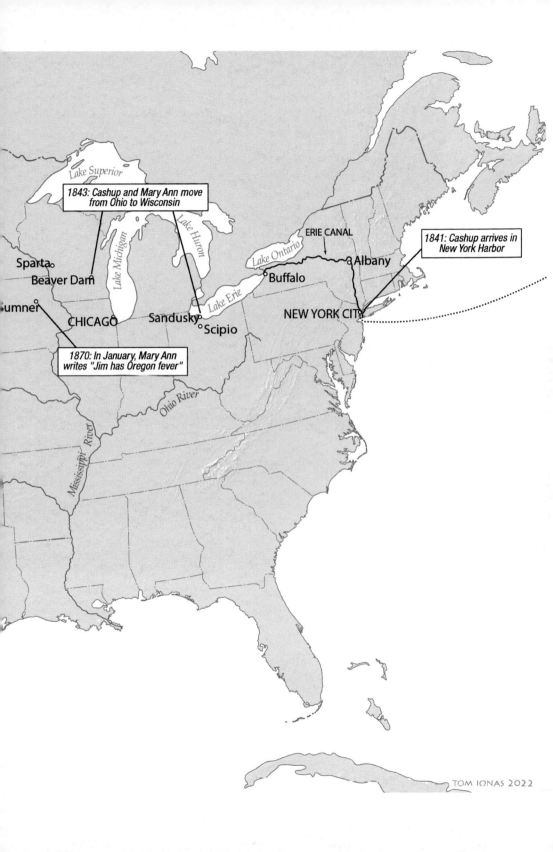

Lake Superior

1843: Cashup and Mary Ann move
from Ohio to Wisconsin

Lake Huron

Lake Michigan

ERIE CANAL

Lake Ontario

1841: Cashup arrives in
New York Harbor

Sparta

Albany

Beaver Dam

Buffalo

Lake Erie

Sumner

CHICAGO

Sandusky

NEW YORK CITY

Scipio

1870: In January, Mary Ann
writes "Jim has Oregon fever"

Ohio River

Mississippi River

TOM IONAS 2022

was searching for "dirt turned for the first time," a farmer's description of soil that has never been farmed or planted by white settlers. A place where his family could join him for the ultimate American West experience he had long sought. On the very edge of settlement.

I first met Randall Johnson, the amateur historian, in the 1970s and I heard him speak about my great-grandfather in 1990. On August 25, 2000, we sat and talked about Cashup for hours. It was as close to meeting Cashup as I could get. That is when Randall told me how he viewed Cashup's incessant wanderings: "My own feeling is he decided, 'I'll know where I want to go when I get there.'"

He was about to get there, yes. But Cashup's looming odyssey did not go as planned.

FOUR

MARY ANN SAYS "NO MORE"

"In search of the green fields just over the hill."
KARL P. ALLEN, *PULLMAN HERALD* NEWSPAPER EDITOR

THE PALOUSE IS UNLIKE ANY place you have ever seen on Earth. They say the magic of the Palouse will slowly sink its claws into your heart and never let go.

Its endless rolling hills are mesmerizing, undulating as far as the eye can see, sloping gracefully, romantically. When the low sun hits the sides of the countless hills, you want to gasp aloud. It is hard to decide whether the sunrises are more beautiful than the sunsets, whether the new season is more beautiful than the last. Indeed, my mom and dad always reminded me while growing up near the Palouse in the 1960s that "the best things in life are free." And a Palouse landscape is surely one of them.

The Palouse lies roughly between present-day Spokane and Walla Walla, between the foothills of northern Idaho and the rocky scablands of central Washington. Depending on who is doing the measuring, the Palouse encompasses up to 19,000 square miles and is sliced by several roaring rivers and a multitude of streams.

Amusingly, even longtime Playboy photographer David Chen, who made a career out of photographing other kinds of curves, called the hills of the Palouse "sexy." Modern-day wheat farmers see money in those hills. Soil scientists see a freak of nature's fertility. Topsoil, often merely a few feet deep in many farming regions, is commonly 30–40 feet deep on the Palouse and can reach an almost inconceivable 240 feet deep—a fact that astonishes experts around the world. It took a long time to create: During the ebb of the last ice age, several hundred miles to the east, the Missoula ice dam broke cataclysmically time and again, allowing the largest sudden flows of water that geologic science has ever found. And then the real magic happened. Over millennia, winds blew the fine sediments left by the floods into shapes, forming the rolling hills that look not unlike desert dunes but are instead rich and fertile land.

The ecological diversity was stunning in its natural state, untouched by European settlers, and impacted only by the movement of Native American tribes and wildlife. Bunchgrass clumps covered the landscape from east to west, nestled amid various species of vegetation, giving animals an invaluable habitat that slowly struck a natural balance over hundreds of thousands of seasons. It was far more prairie than forest, with very few trees, making lumbering a major obstacle for early settlers (as James was about to find out).

The size of each hill is not too big and not too small. They range between about a quarter of a mile around up to a circumference of a mile or more, rising a few dozen feet to several hundred. One hill in particular—a butte, actually, and some call it a mountain—rises more than a thousand feet above the surrounding land. Made of quartzite 400 million years old, it protrudes above the rocky basalt foundation, with the silty loess (pronounced "less") at its foot. This butte dominates the landscape like a pyramid peak, which is the name used by the first white people to lay eyes on it. Then it was called Mount Lincoln for a time, after the president's assassination in 1865, according to historian and pioneer journalist Edith Erickson. After an Indian war that defeated Col. Edward Steptoe's forces (a story we will address later), the butte gradually became known by its current name, Steptoe Butte. But the original name is Yasmústus (Palouse), according to acclaimed historian and author Richard Scheuerman. Other tribes have similar pronunciations. Scheuerman recalls a tribal elder told him the word means "where elk live," a mythological place where for centuries Indigenous people went to connect to a spiritual power. Consequently, many Indians referred to the landform as "power mountain."

James knew nothing about this rocky butte at all. But, protruding more than a thousand feet above the surrounding prairie, its power would eventually consume his life. And he was about to lay eyes on it for the very first time.

Traveling from western Oregon, James likely sensed the early moments of the rush inland, including to the Palouse, and it stirred his competitive juices. He was coming to the Upper Country, as the settlers called it then, aboard the *Wide West* steamer, up the Columbia River and eventually to the southwestern edge of the Palouse. (Karl Allen actually wrote the name as *Wild West*, but we found no record of a steamer with such a name, only one called the *Wide West*. So, we conclude that the latter is the steamer Allen intended to mention.) When the steamers could make no more progress up the waterway, he found a way to cover the last 100–150 miles into the heart of the Palouse. Family friend Stokely Clarence Roberts, whose byline was "S. C. Roberts," wrote that by "securing two good mules, one to ride and one to pack necessary supplies," James "made the journey alone."

James was now on the Palouse for the first time. Seeing it. Feeling it. Listening to it. Smelling it. Getting to know it. As he lay drifting to sleep that first night on the lonely trek inland in the summer of 1872, likely bedded under the warm night sky, gazing at the stars above, what might he have been thinking? Did he ask himself: "What am I seeking? When do I stop? How will I know I have found my place? What will happen when I bring my family here? Am I safe? Will my family be safe? Am I simply too far into the wilderness? I'm already a grandfather and in my mid-fifties. Am I up to this?" Did he reflect on his early life in England, building the Dover Tunnel under Shakespeare Mountain or assisting a military officer around aristocratic Britain, while lying in an area of unending bunchgrass where few white people had ever set foot? Did he contemplate the ultimate question: "Why?"

As James arrived in a central area of the Palouse, he caught his first glimpse of Steptoe Butte. We will never know whether his initial encounter was barely a second thought or whether there was a gasp and a pause as he strode up or around a hill to reveal the view of the conical sentinel. Indeed, Steptoe was later often referred to as the Silent Sentinel. And less than ten years before James's trek to the Palouse, a government stagecoach driver named M. V. Elliott ran his horses, cargo, and passengers past Steptoe when it was called Pyramid Peak. Elliott's daughter said in a letter that her father wrote to his entire family back in Missouri about this startling butte as he drove the stage between Fort Dodge, Kansas, and Fort Walla Walla and Fort Colville in the early 1860s. So drawn to the area was the Elliott family that they, too, joined the pioneer settlers there.

Many of us have had a significant moment in our own lives: a first glimpse of our future spouse, of our dream house, of a new city destined to become home. James saw Steptoe Butte, no doubt, because the mountain is impossible not to see. Of all the mesmerizing hilltops of the Palouse, it is the grandest by far. James chose his plot of land about fifteen miles west of the wondrous landform. Even at such a distance, the butte seems like it is just arm's-length away. And when the sun set that first evening on the Palouse, Steptoe Butte would no doubt have been bathed in its famed orange glow.

Steptoe Butte is lit by a beautiful Palouse sunset. When James Davis arrived in the Palouse alone on a mule in 1871, he first laid eyes on the butte that would consume him. Photograph by Daymon Marple.

It is anyone's guess how James selected his plot of land to claim. Knowing what I know now about my great-grandfather, I imagine he evaluated hundreds of locations to call home. And he would have been focused on his number one priority: land for farming small grains and livestock. James knew the land was fertile here, but he had no idea just how fertile. Such knowledge would come later. Pioneer family letters later described the plot a few miles southwest of present-day Thornton, on the way to a small town called Sunset. (The town did not yet exist, of course, and is still very small.) Standing on what is likely the land James chose (somewhere near where the Sunset Road now intersects with Washboard Road), it is easy to see why he chose it: it is a beautiful stretch of rolling hills and wide flat valley sliced by Cottonwood Creek, with a few shrubs dotting the water's edge. The creek's path has meandered and changed over time: it is

One of the earliest known photographs of the town of Colfax, Washington, in 1878. The Palouse River can be seen running through town. It was the nearest town to Cashup's growing empire a few miles north. From Northwest Museum of Arts and Culture (MAC), Virgil McCroskey Collection, MS 147, Box 2, Folder 8

now little more than a narrow channel as valuable farmland has encroached on its edges and consumed most of its flow of water. As beautiful as a mirage? You could say that, as James was about to find out.

By this time, several hundred settlers had staked claims throughout the Palouse, and villages—clusters of homes, really—would soon form. Two years before James's arrival, a settler named James Perkins arrived in a rocky valley about thirty miles southeast of where James staked his claim. He founded a settlement there and named the fledgling town Belleville, after his girlfriend. When he found another love, he changed the name to Colfax, in honor of the Ulysses S. Grant's Vice President Schuyler Colfax.

Of course, for seventy years or more, whites had travelled into and through the Palouse but almost never stayed permanently. Lewis and Clark had scouted near the Palouse on their historic trip in 1805 (nearby Lewiston, Idaho, and Clarkston, Washington, were later named in their honor). French fur trappers and traders knew the region well, especially Joseph LaRoque who, in 1823, was among the first white settlers in what is now eastern Washington, after marrying the daughter of a Walla Walla chief. (Jake LaRoque, a direct descendant of Joseph's, would become my Sigma Chi fraternity brother.) In 1860, a youthful Lt. John Mullan and his crew completed the first major road over the Rocky Mountains into the greater Palouse region, connecting Fort Walla Walla with Fort Benton in Montana. It later became the crucial "highway" for the military—and, eventually, for civilian use—and can still be seen in places today. Before becoming Mullan's highway, much of the route had been an Indian trail. Today, parts of Interstate 90 follow its path.

Whitman County was established in 1870, two years before James's arrival, when the census counted just over a hundred white settlers in Union Flats, a central area of present-day Whitman County, where new arrivals gathered to settle.

Having staked his land claim, James retuned to McMinnville that summer to fetch his family and possessions and return to the Upper Country. He took his clan from McMinnville to the Palouse, nearly 400 miles, by covered wagon and horses, rather than via several steamers up the Columbia River, which would have required a passenger ticket for each member of his family and payment for all their possessions. At this point, he may very well have been short on cash, based on his McMinnville letter. This may have been the leg of their journey referenced often by others as their overland "covered wagon" journey. In Julia Davis Eckhart's notes recounting her father's family trip when he was a boy from McMinnville to the Palouse, she said "the trip was rough and tough with lots of obstacles [that] lay in their path to the Palouse hills." She added that Ed, her father, mentioned an Indian scare during this specific trip to the Palouse, but she couldn't recall the incident. Amy Charlotte Davis, one of the young children in the back of the family wagon, told her family many years later that Klamath Indians encountered along the way peered into the covered wagon, terrifying her and the other kids inside. It underscores, if nothing else, how truly vulnerable white families were while traveling through tribal homelands where they were often viewed—quite accurately—as invaders.

The end of the journey marked a big moment for James Davis. He was taking his family to his plot of land, the new home he had sought for so many years. On arrival, according to several accounts, he discovered that George Newmeyer, a man in his early twenties, had "jumped" James's claim, elbowing the Davis family out of the land James had so carefully surveyed in that beautiful flat valley along Cottonwood Creek. What was he to do? Having lost his chosen spot in the fall, with winter looming just a few weeks away, James not only had to find a new plot of land but also secure shelter for his family before the first snows hit the Palouse.

"Squatting" on unsurveyed land meant one needed to be present on the land to claim it in advance of the government surveying the area and arranging for formal homestead claims to be filed. The practice was not entirely unusual in the rush to settle the west. As S. C. Roberts writes, "land was plentiful though all un-surveyed, and Mr. Davis, nothing daunted, left his family for two weeks at Torrance Bridge, some 10 miles west of Colfax, while he sought out another location, choosing finally, a place farther down the valley, exercising squatter's rights again to be the first settled at [present day] St. John." James laid claim to "three quarter sections of land."

The exact location of James's land claim has remained a mystery. Present-day historians in St. John think that the Davis family established just south of town. Jim Gisselberg, a farmer a few miles east of St. John and a descendant from a pioneer family, says his father told him that Hastings Gulch on their land was named by James Davis himself, after his hometown in England. And Hastings Creek runs through the gulch in wet weather. With so many hills and creeks and gulches in the area, James likely lived in or very near Hastings Gulch. However, Gisselberg also notes that a family named Hastings had farmed nearby many years ago. So, that tantalizing clue remains unsettled.

James's family arrived in anticipation of witnessing a "promised land," based on James's magnificent descriptions. Instead, Roberts writes, Davis offered them housing "at the foot of a low hill, in a habitation part dug-out and part sod walls built of . . . turf. There were two large rooms with a partition of sacked flour hauled from Walla Walla." The new home was merely a sod house: large squares of soil permeated by grass roots harvested from the ground, used like large dirt bricks, an earthy edifice tucked into a hillside. "Soddies," as these structures were called, were common on prairies in the American West and parts of northern Europe. They usually had a door and windows and some sort of stove inside to cook on and to keep their interior warm. In her family history, Julia Davis Eckhart said "grandfather Cashup Davis built the first sod house where St. John, Washington now stands."

Given James's experience at design, engineering, and construction, along with his supply of chutzpah, any sod home he built probably offered a lot more than most. It must have been well built, as Roberts reported that the Davis family and their neighbors survived a strong earthquake while hunkering down inside. "The walls shook and dirt rattled down from the roof. On inquiry, every neighbor reported a similar visitation. The explanation came when the Portland Oregonian [newspaper] gave a detailed account of an earthquake over the region." Geologic records indicate the earthquake hit on December 14, 1872, just 150 miles west of where he built the sod house. It was a very strong quake, estimated at a magnitude of 6.5–7.0.

Using details provided many years later by James's daughter Mary Ann, Roberts writes, "There he held three quarter sections of land [480 acres], living in the dug-out two years while building up a fine herd of more than a hundred cattle and fattening them on grain hay since the marketing of grain was prohibitive for lack of roads and distance to the boat landings on the Snake river." At some point, James and his family moved out of the sod house and into an impressive ten-room house with outbuildings, a barn, and a corral he built himself on the land. The larger family home was the first house built near the community that would become St. John just a few years later.

James's house is something townspeople still talk about to this day in the tidy, small farming town. As the house was built more than 150 years ago, no trace of the building has been found. Lydia Smith, president of the St. John Historical Society in 2021 and other long-time locals believe the property was located about a mile and a half east of St. John in Pleasant Valley. As I look around at Pleasant Valley, I can see why my great-grandfather may have felt it was a magnificent place to claim. It is a beautiful area and it no doubt looked very much the same when James lived here. On the far side of the valley is a stream, Pleasant Valley Creek, that meanders down the flatlands where low green trees cuddle up to its banks.

Standing there, I tried to put myself into James's thinking back then. The low hills on the opposite valley wall by the stream indeed looked like an ideal place to build a sod house set against an exposed hillside, as Roberts described it. A walk along the stream and a close examination of the long low hillside turned up no remnants of the family structure, of course. After all, a sod house quickly returns to the earth.

Still standing there, I get shivers realizing that I am in the valley where James and his clan probably began their long tenure on the Palouse and laid the foundation for the start of my life and the others in the extended Davis family, many of whom continue to live in the region. Perhaps somewhere under the tall stands of wheat we might find the remnants of a foundation, or a well, or metal tools. Such a discovery, though, will have to wait for another day.

Settling In and Starting a New Life

To start raising crops and livestock on the fertile soil of the Palouse, James began by turning the bunchgrass. Surrounded by abundant grassland, pioneers rarely had to buy feed for livestock, except for perhaps two to three weeks during winter. Such a practice was a huge financial advantage for ranchers in that era. Indeed, it enabled large-scale ranchers to drive massive herds out west without needing to haul feed.

The Davis family's herd of cattle grew to one hundred, which was impressive for a newcomer, according to the family notes. As fences had not been built at that point, livestock were free to roam all year long while they ate the grasses and got fat. The downside of having no fences was that owners had to spend considerable effort to find their livestock after the animals wandered away.

Optimistically, James wrote to his adult son William in the Midwest, inviting him to come to the Palouse to live. It is the second of the two James Davis letters known to exist and gives us a window into his world in his own words. The letter is full of fascinating details of daily life, of the economics of farming and ranching in the new West.

Whitman County, Friday, January 5, 1873

Dear Son: I received your letter and check dated December 15, and was very glad to hear from you and all of you. We are all well and in good spirits, now you wanted to know something about this country. In the first place it is a vast rolling prairie. In some places it is hilly with beautiful valleys with beautiful springs and streams of water. The country is one vast pasturage of grass. Its fattening qualities are unsurpassed by any in the world.

It matures on the ground. Cattle are fat all the year. I have eight horses, and I have not fed any grain since I have been here and not more than two-hundred-pounds of hay and do not expect to feed any, although it snows now, but we expect it to go off in a few days now. These valleys run from 50 to 160 acres and from 5 to 50 miles long.

There are some claims on each side of me just as good as mine, that I think are worth money. They are very pretty and level but they will be gone in the spring, if not before. The country is fast settling up. I have just got home my seed wheat and oats. I paid ninety cents a bushel for wheat, seventy-five cents for oats and two cents a pound for potatoes, the best potatoes I ever ate in my life. I expect to break up a hundred acres this spring. Timber is scarce in some places, in some it is plenty. I have to go eight miles some places, but you can get timber and prairie together.

I wrote the first column yesterday when it was snowing. Today it is all going away. My horses are all gone off to grazing and are getting fat. If any of you are coming here, you had better come as soon as you can or else the best claims will be taken up. Our spring opens about the first of February.

Immigration will be coming in here very soon now. If any of you come here you had better take a ticket to Colton, a station on the Northern Railroad.

If David and you or Andrew or a part of you come, make it an object to buy a wagon if you wish and come through on the stage route. If David should come, he can ship his goods to Walula [sic] on the Columbia River, Washington

Territory. It will cost him about $80 to $100 to ship 100 pounds. If they are well packed. The boxes must be well packed and closely pressed. The larger the bulk the more it will cost. When you get them shipped you must get a bill of lading, and put iron bands on your clothing and bedding. So much for your freight. Now for yourselves, your best way to come is to take a ticket to Walla Walla, you will come on the railroad to a place called Helton. Then you take the stage to Walla Walla. You must not bring any trunks by stage, one man brought a trunk weighing sixty pounds and it cost him $40. If David comes, you had better send what things you have with him around to Portland, and now if you come and should not like it I do not want you to blame me.

Now you figure on 500 sheep and their increase for seven years, even calling the wool at seventy-five cents a head, and the increase one dollar in a country where you do not have to feed them all the year, with thousands of acres of pasture without even to pay taxes on, then you look at cows, your increase and your butter at $40 a week, and this in gold besides your calves, say fifteen calves out of twenty cows at $10 a calf, then your hogs from your grain and milk and your land for nothing nearly.

Cattle and sheep must be high for years, the home market will demand the increase for years. Sheep are after shearing about $2 a head. Cows from $25 to $45. A two-year old calf is as large as your three year olds, and make splendid cows. Now tell the girls both of them we would all of us very much like to see them and their little babies. We have not heard from David or Andrew for a long time. I expect they write to Ferdanand [sic] and Ed for their information. I expect they are at Walla Walla which is 100 miles from me now.

If any of you come we will meet you with teams at Walla Walla, if you let us know when you start and what way you come and your mother and children at home want to see you and all.

They send their kind love to you all, and likewise myself.

James Davis

When I read this letter written by my great-grandfather in his own hand, I feel so firmly that family was exceedingly important to him. He was a tough pioneer in a culture where fathers and husbands were often dictatorial. Yet my great-grandfather showed a kind heart for his children, and, no doubt, his grandchildren too—even if he was also tough with them. Here is where his legacy starts to form. His sons and daughters were vitally important to him. Did he see them as his legacy? I don't think so. I believe Cashup saw his legacy in other things, other achievements, over the next hill.

Despite sending that warm invitation to William to rejoin the family, James decided to move again. This time, he planned to leave the United States. After two or three years of life on the Palouse, on his oasis in Pleasant Valley, James loaded up the family and began his search for—well, for whatever it was he was searching. On this move, James was taking the family overland by covered wagon to Canada, into the territory Queen Victoria had named "British Columbia" less than fifteen years prior. Roberts reported: "After three years at St. John, Davis sold out, having decided to move to British Columbia, inspired, no doubt by the prospect of settling among his countrymen there."

Imagine the conversation with Mary Ann. They had moved from Ohio to LeRoy, Wisconsin, then to Sparta, Wisconsin, and on to Iowa; then across the western territories to Oregon to start a farm on the Palouse. And now they were going north of the US border to Canada. When was James going to stop moving?

In 1874, likely in the spring, their wagon headed out toward the eastern horizon. The magnificent Okanagan Valley 175 miles directly north had an ideal climate for fruit trees and other farmland—although so did the Palouse. It is unclear where James intended to go in British Columbia or why. There were probably just as many British immigrants in the US Pacific Northwest as in British Columbia. And, other than the "no doubt" conjecture offered by Roberts, there is no direct evidence that James sought to live alongside his fellow countrymen. Besides, he was an American now. Nevertheless, to reach the more travelled routes that would get them north to the border, James headed southeast from St. John, where he could pick up established wagon roads. By happenstance, the route southeast took the family within spitting distance of Steptoe Butte.

Mary Ann possessed a combination of toughness and heart. James was determined, brilliant, and stubborn. The Davis caravan camped on the first night near Steptoe Butte, where the trail from their now abandoned home intersected with the popular territorial wagon road. And it was here that Mary Ann, no doubt exasperated, took a stand of epic proportion. Life with a strong-willed, confident man—described as determined and domineering, constantly in search of the greener grass just over the next hill—finally became too much for her. "After one day on the road, his good wife, weary of repeated wandering, went on a mild form of strike with the result the first night's camping place bec[oming] a permanent home," recalled Roberts. Johnson's written lore, clearly using Roberts as his source, tells the story: "One can almost hear her: 'Stop the wagon, James!'" (although her letters show that she called him Jim rather than James).

Regardless of what Mary Ann actually said, the new journey ended abruptly. Oh my, that was another conversation that descendants wish they could have heard. It certainly cemented respect for Mary Ann among many future generations of Davises, as we will see.

I feel she likely scolded him. No, no, she likely chewed his ass. Deservedly so, as I see it all these years later. Now, let me be transparent about my feelings regarding this defining moment for James and Mary Ann. I hesitate to use a swear word here because I want to keep this story dignified and told with respect, as James deserves. But, among the many traits James handed down to his descendants was frank talk. Say what you mean. So, with your understanding, I will leave in the phrase she chewed his ass. Because I think she did, without question.

With Mary Ann's ruling final, the family's latest trek stopped right there, in the shadow of Steptoe Butte. She was now in her late forties and James about sixty—roughly twelve years apart. I feel she was a combination of toughness and heart to a high degree. Clearly, James respected her. After her impassioned remarks, he never put his family on the trail again. Well, for the most part— as you will soon read.

While Mary Ann was becoming a Palouse pioneer, her ancestors were a truly American pioneering family, having arrived in this country on January 20, 1686, according to her family documents. She was perhaps the ninth generation of her family in America, a striking achievement in a still-young nation. Her ancestors George and Sarah Shoemaker married in Heidelberg, Germany, in 1662. With six children, they sailed to America aboard the ship *Jeffries* during the winter of 1685. Before they could reach the shores of "the wilderness country," as family papers called it, George and his father died onboard. There is no information about the cause. But Sarah was left to shepherd her six children as they landed on the shores of the Delaware River in Philadelphia. Such a challenging episode sowed the seeds of toughness in her family. A Shoemaker family historian named Benjamin H. Shoemaker III wrote that she had been of the

Mennonite faith and was converted to the Quakers by William Penn himself.

Generations later, Mary Ann, the eighth of ten siblings, was certainly the Shoemaker who travelled farther west from Pennsylvania and Ohio than the others. Now here she sat on that covered wagon, less than a day on the trail, declaring she had had enough searching for their Eden. This place would be their Eden. And little did either of them know at the time, but she was absolutely correct. It was the most fortuitous decision the family ever made. (Or shall we say, the most fortuitous decision Mary Ann ever made.)

Throughout this story, we frequently describe a place as " . . . near present-day . . . " and then name a city or town. This time, the spot where they stopped can be described as "in the present-day small town of Cashup." Little did they know that the land on which they settled would eventually bear his name, a nickname James had yet to acquire.

The family's youngest child and my grandfather, Charley, was on that wagon. He was just seven years old when his mother put an end to the family's travels. In a letter full of family history written in the 1930s, Charley's wife, Grace Davis (my grandmother), describes the spot where they stopped as "a lovely fertile valley with a fine view of Steptoe Butte." Fertile, indeed. So fortuitous was this spontaneous decision to stop and seek the land under their feet that Roberts wrote it was "a tract probably unsurpassed in fertility in all the Inland Empire," a term for the vast region that stretches east from the Cascade Mountains to the Rockies. James soon found out just how big the crop yields would be on this patch of land.

Grace made handwritten notes that avowed, in nearly the very spot where the family stopped, that this is the place where they would plant their new lives, future, and new crops. Farming remained their major focus. They started with 640 acres of land owned by a railroad company, although James told a newspaper

Charley Davis, the youngest son of James and Mary Ann, with his wife Grace, son Aubrey, and daughter Vivian, 1915. Aubrey is Gordon's father. From the collection of James Martin.

reporter later that he "occupied" it for four years before purchasing it (he eventually acquired 1600 acres). Wheat, barley, oats, fruit trees, and livestock became their livelihood. It was an astonishing farming operation in the Palouse bunchgrass. Their farming and ranching took off. They earned a great deal of respect and money from it. But that wasn't all. Always thinking ahead, James realized this spot was in an ideal location on the territorial road along a burgeoning stagecoach line. It was located between Walla Walla and Spokane Falls, the two big cities in the region at the time. James could see that passing stage drivers would need a place to stop to water their horses and to buy food and drink for themselves and their passengers.

The letter from Grace continues: "There, James S. Davis took up 1600 acres of railroad land at $2.60 per acre. He built two houses, one dwelling, the other a large store with a dance hall and dining room. They 'kept travel' as they called it in those days. When the stage came thru[, it] made a regular stop once a day going between Colfax and Spokane." The home he built was a ten-room, two-story house, identical to his St. John home. His barn was big, 40 feet by 100 feet.

In this new location, James Davis established his place in history. His legend soon built from there, especially since he was about to get a new name: Cashup.

FIVE

THE SETTLERS AND THE INDIANS

Whenever the white man treats the Indian as they treat each other, then we will have no more wars. We shall all be alike—brothers of one father and one mother with one sky above us and one country around us and one government for all.

CHIEF JOSEPH, NIIMÍIPUU (NEZ PERCE) TRIBE

MARY ANN FEARED SHE WOULD be killed. She was on the run. She wrote: "Dear children, I once more take my pencil for I've not got a pen. We are fleeing from the Indians. They have broke out and are killing settlers, about 40 miles from our house and people are fleeing for their lives. The roads are full of people leaving their homes and everything behind. It's an awful thing."

With four of her children in her care, Mary Ann scribbled the letter from a town called Tucannon, Washington, on July 22, 1877, perhaps fearing that it would be the last thing she would ever get to say to her older children living back in the Midwest. She tried to finish the letter quickly so she could hand it off to the US mail carrier who was riding right past her. But she couldn't finish. She had more to write, so she handed it off to the next carrier. Postal communications in 1877 meant her children in the Midwest would not read the letter for twenty days or so, followed by anguished waiting about whether or not Mary Ann and their siblings were still alive.

Mary Ann's heartfelt letter to her children on July 22, 1877, during her flight from the danger the pioneers perceived when regional Native tribes, primarily the Nez Perce led by Chief Joseph, rebelled against the US government. From SPC 980-0131; Archives & Special Collections, Eastern Washington University, Cheney, WA.

Mary Ann had special personal reason to fear for her life. While fleeing, she must have been thinking about her mother who, as a child in Pennsylvania in the late 1700s, was the sole survivor of an Indian massacre, according to Shoemaker family papers. Her mother grew up, married, and gave birth to ten children, including Mary Ann. After leaving her wealthy and comfortable family back East, Mary Ann had chosen to venture west with her husband to unsettled land, and now found herself on the run from Indians. Frightening! She surely must have been questioning their decision to come so far west.

Cashup was stubborn. Even with the belief that Indians were on the attack, he refused to leave their home. He was very good with a rifle but, even more so, it would be entirely consistent with what we know about Cashup if he believed he could reason with Native Americans who were allegedly in armed conflict with the U.S. Army.

As Mary Ann and the younger kids fled, Cashup stayed behind with his son Clarence, 17, to try to protect the house, farm, crops, and livestock, according to Mary Ann's panicked letter. Ferdinand, she wrote, would join his father and brother after he helped move another family to safety.

With Mary Ann were her son Ed, 24, and the younger children: Mary, 15, Charlotte ("Lottie"), 13, and Charley, 10. They hurried more than sixty miles southwestward toward Fort Walla Walla, where they felt they could hide in safety with other fleeing pioneers. When she wrote that letter, she had just crossed the Snake River at one of the commercial ferry crossings and likely felt a degree of safety on its southern bank. She wrote that she stopped short about forty miles from Fort Walla Walla and camped in a grove. She was poised to continue fleeing if word came the Indians were coming in their direction. Even if they remained physically unharmed, she feared the family would lose everything they had worked so hard to achieve—their home, the animals, the fields. "I never saw crops look better," she wrote that day. You can almost hear her weep in her letter. "We have the prettiest farm in the country. Everybody says so that passes by our place. I think so too. I had the nicest garden and everything in it and had to leave it and go without. I will tell you more when I write again." She wrote partly in past tense.

She worried about their one hundred head of hogs, one hundred head of cattle, and thirty-two horses and colts. "The Indians are killing hogs and cattle by the hundreds and driving off all the horses they can find. We expect to hear of our house being burned and everything destroyed," she wrote. Another woman, Barbara Jane Matlock McRay, who had also fled to Tucannon (they likely knew each other), recounted rumors that there were "blood thirsty Indians on the war path . . . cutting off the tongues of children and raping the women." Mary Ann was getting her information from the same source: cowboys galloping past them. "They had 3 battles with the Indians and the Indians beat twice," Mary Ann wrote, "and butchered the soldiers, and had a war dance."

The settlers called this event the Indian Scare of 1877, which was precipitated when some elements of the Nez Perce Indians and allied tribes clashed with the US military as remnants of the tribes were being physically forced onto a small reservation. Without reliable communication, rumors spread that settlers, too, were being attacked. With little or no confirmation of what was happening, citizens in eastern Washington panicked.

Historian Richard Scheuerman writes that pioneers in the area hurriedly constructed forts in the towns of Colfax, Palouse, and Spangle—a terrifying endeavor. Cashup wanted his son Ed to help Mary Ann and the younger children reach the additional level of safety behind the walls of Fort Walla Walla.

Mary Ann stayed put in Tucannon and relied on the daily passage of mail carriers and others to keep her informed about what was happening back in the center of the Palouse. She also wrote something rather cryptic, as if she wanted to preserve a memory for her children if the worst were to befall her. "If I go to Walla Walla, I will have our pictures taken and send them to you."

And then, near the end of her letter, she wrote: "I guess there won't be much more now. My health is poor, my heart troubles me. I sure hope I get better soon. Dear children, shall we ever meet here again."

And then there is the other side of the story.

The perspective of the Niimíipuu tribe was profoundly different from that held by many white settlers, military men, and US government officials. A closer examination of the historical record underscores this disparity. No children's tongues were cut off nor were women raped. No soldiers were butchered on the Palouse, neither were livestock slaughtered.

The region was populated by a number of tribes, including the Niimíipuu, the Palouse (or Palus), the Walla Wallas, the Cayuses, the Yakamas, the Spokanes, the Coeur d'Alenes, and others. To understand what actually led up to the 1877 scare, we must look back a few years to examine the US government's mistreatment of Indians.

1855

At the 1855 Walla Walla Council, twenty-two years before Mary Ann wrote her letter, the federal government convinced some of the Nez Perce and others to sign a treaty removing them from their homelands. The Nez Perce were forced to move off their ancestral homeland of thirteen million acres and live on a reservation about half the original size. A number of northwest Indian treaties of that era, spearheaded by Washington's territorial governor Isaac Stevens, were written in English and verbalized in tribal languages that the signers often did not speak—a fatal legal flaw by today's standards. The treaties gave them rights to hunt, fish, pasture, and roam in their "usual and accustomed places." The diminished Nez Perce territory included the area that is present-day Lewiston, Idaho. The treaty declared that white settlers were not allowed to come onto their reservation without permission.

The "agreement" led to the periodic eruption of numerous skirmishes, fights, battles, and all-out wars between US soldiers and the displaced Native peoples as white settlement continued to increase exponentially. Indeed, the times when one could ride on a horse all day without seeing another settler were long over. The new arrivals snapped up the suddenly available land to homestead. The forced displacement and the tensions it created prompted the US government to plan the Mullan Road to better mobilize the military at Fort Walla Walla, Fort Colville, and Fort Benton in Montana.

Walla Walla Council with Washington Governor Stevens and the local Native tribes, May 1855. At this council and others like it, Tribes were coerced into signing treaties that took away their lands and their rights to live as their ancestors had for thousands of years. Washington State Historical Society.

1858

Among the most well-known of those Indian battles was the 1858 Steptoe Disaster, also called the Battle of Pine Creek or the Battle of Tohotonimme. Steptoe Butte, the site of Cashup's future legend, was made famous not because of a battle on the butte (it did not happen that way, despite numerous erroneous historical accounts) but because Steptoe Butte was named after Lt. Col. Edward Steptoe, who led the US military to defeat in the battle a few miles to the north near Rosalia, Washington. Lt. Col. Steptoe assembled 159 soldiers from Fort Walla Walla to travel north, ostensibly to investigate the alleged murder of two white miners who had encroached onto a reservation (the murders may not have actually occurred), but also to reassure anxious settlers with a strong US military presence. By marching onto an Indian reservation, however, the government violated the treaty. An angry coalition of tribes gathered as many as 1,000 men, vastly outnumbering Steptoe and his troops. The tribes hit Steptoe's army hard—what has been described as a ten-hour series of running skirmishes—before nightfall paused the fighting. Overnight, Steptoe, with essential help from Nez Perce Chief Timothy, silently guided his troops through an undefended enemy line and retreated to the west. It was a wise move, because Steptoe had issued each of his fighting men just forty rounds of ammunition. Any further fighting and the army would have quickly run out of bullets.

In a haunting retaliation three months later against the Yakama, Spokane, Palouse, and Coeur d'Alene tribes, Steptoe's commander Col. George Wright ordered fresh troops to battle in several small engagements. Don Cutler notes that "Wright's advance devolved into a bloody and vindictive march featuring hangings, burned villages, lies and coercion." Indeed, his furious helmsmanship intended the tribes' surrender or they would face "extermination." To drive the message home, Wright's men slaughtered nearly 800 horses belonging to the Palouse tribe, leading them to suffer starvation conditions during the winter.

1860

Despite the treaty, a stream of miners in 1860 began entering Indian land near present-day Lewiston, where gold had been discovered. The US government did nothing to stop the violation. Farmers and ranchers followed, churning up the bunchgrass and altering the ecosystem on which the tribes depended for their very existence. The land was their food source, their church, and their home.

1869

Native land ownership shrunk even more in 1869 when a group of Nez Perce was coerced into giving away 90% of their already shrunken reservation, leaving them with just 750,000 acres east of Lewiston. Those who signed the questionable deal may not have even represented the Nez Perce, leading many to simply not accept it.

1877

The situation worsened in May 1877, when Gen. Oliver Howard, known as "the Christian General," gave the remaining Nez Perce tribal members 30 days to move onto their remaining 750,000 acres or be forcefully moved. With just days to go before the deadline, 600 or so Nez Perce gathered to accede to General Howard's demands. During the ceremonies at the gathering, several enraged Nez Perce youths raided nearby homesteads, killing four innocent white men and wounding another.

A great distance to the east, largely in Montana, an army of 1,500 US soldiers, civilian volunteers, and Indian scouts pursued and attacked at least 700 Nez Perce men, women, and children, led by the legendary Chief Joseph, from June to October 1877. The US Army lost 125 men. The tribe lost over one hundred men, women, and children; 150–200 Indians fled to Canada and 418 men, women, and children surrendered. Most of those who surrendered were taken on trains to jail in Leavenworth, Kansas, or to live with unfamiliar tribes in the sweltering heat of Oklahoma. This is when Chief Joseph uttered his well-known line, "I will fight no more forever." It was considered at the time as the last breath of the great Nez Perce.

Many historians and other authorities believe the American government set out on a concerted effort for generations to destroy or "fix" the first peoples of North America because it perceived them as heathens and savages who needed the influence of white culture to save them.

"When a white army battles Indians and wins, it is called a great victory, but if they lose it is called a massacre," said Chiksika, a Shawnee war chief in the 1700s. It makes me think of my

Chief Joseph, Nez Perce tribal leader, in a photograph by Edward Curtis. Undated. From Chris Cardozo of Cardozo Fine Art, courtesy of Julie.

boyhood watching Westerns and cowboy movies on TV. The American people were fed propaganda about Native Americans for 150 years or more. I see now these Indigenous people were grossly mistreated, lied to and so rightly fought to defend their freedom. It breaks my heart.

As Indians were systematically removed from their ancestral land to "vacant land" in other parts of America, a countless number of them marched to their deaths. Charles R. Hicks, Tsalagi (Cherokee) vice chief, speaking of the Trail of Tears:

"We are now about to take our leave and kind farewell to our native land, the country the Great Spirit gave our Fathers, we are on the eve of leaving that country that gave us birth, it is with sorrow we are forced by the white man to quit the scenes of our childhood. . . . we bid farewell to it and all we hold dear."

In the weeks following the Nez Perce War, the *New York Times* wrote an editorial that declared, "On our part, the war was in its origin and motive nothing short of a gigantic blunder and a crime."

This rare photo, taken during the 1877 "wars," shows Nez Perce on horseback in Lapwai, Idaho, including Chief Joseph, White Bird, and Looking Glass. Courtesy of the Northwest Museum of Arts and Culture, Joel E. Ferris Research Archives; Roy Berk Collection, American Indians of the Pacific Northwest Images, L94-7.105

Mary Ann and Cashup Were Safe

Despite the scare, it is probable that Mary Ann and Cashup and the rest of the settlers on the Palouse did not see any Indian violence in the hot summer of 1877. It all happened hundreds of miles away. The fear and panic that Cashup and Mary Ann experienced during the scare must have made them feel conflicted. In every place where Cashup made a home during his life in America, Native Americans were all around him: from Ohio less than a generation after white settlement to a Wisconsin town surrounded by tribes being pushed from their homelands; to Iowa, Oregon, and the Palouse. Cashup, who often demonstrated a kind soul and a friendly heart, by all accounts respected the Indigenous people. British-born Cashup, growing up where there were no Indigenous societies per se, saw himself as a new arrival in America.

Many derogatory references exist about the Native Americans in the historical record of the Palouse and elsewhere. But some references make it clear that many of the pioneers got along well with local Indians and that the conflicts were largely between the tribes and the US government.

Cashup's view toward the Indigenous people of the Palouse is illuminated in a couple of paragraphs included in *An Illustrated History of the State of Washington* (1894). In the troubled relations between the US military and the tribes, Cashup did not take sides. In 1878, the year after Mary Ann fled the Indian Scare, Cashup hauled food supplies to the military troops at the new fort in Coeur d'Alene, which was about sixty miles away and still a few years away from being named Fort Sherman. *The Illustrated History* reads: "He fed the officers from Fort Coeur d'Alene, which was in process of construction when he came, and also met the wants of the Indians. On account of his fair, honest and hospitable treatment of the Indians, they looked upon him as a friend even in time[s] of trouble, and it seemed that even then he was in no danger; and, when he went away to the reservation, the Indians kept the stock off his grain." Standing guard to keep livestock from crushing the crops suggests the Indians' respect toward Cashup and his family. And it makes it clear that Cashup conducted business with them. Pushed out of their vast homelands and onto reservations, the tribes no longer had easy access to food as they had for many thousands of years. They often did not have enough to eat. There are pioneer accounts of Indians randomly approaching houses begging for food. Some settlers angrily slammed the door, but others helped them out.

The article in the *Illustrated History* continues: "On one occasion Spokane Indian Agent McIntire wrote to Mr. Davis that the Indians were out of provisions, and wanted to know whether he would furnish supplies and wait for his pay." It is unclear which tribe or tribes McIntire meant, but his wording suggests those to the north of the Palouse. McIntire was now asking Cashup, who got his nickname by refusing deals without cash up front, to do exactly the opposite. And it was a large transaction with no certainty of quick payment and no collateral whatsoever.

"On receiving a reply in the affirmative, 150 ponies were sent down, which Mr. Davis loaded to their utmost capacity, and sent back. So heavily laden were the ponies that, in crossing a creek with steep banks, they could not get up without assistance and the [female Native Americans] had to go out into the water and lift on them buy [sic] their tails."

"The first in charity always," reported the *Spokane Falls Review* in 1892, "is an exclamation that goes up from all who have had experience with Mr. Davis. At a time when the Indians were out of food he was the person to aid them."

Cashup had now come full circle: pioneers, including Cashup, were displacing Indians, yet he demonstrated heart. When he docked in New York harbor, newspapers often cited the famous phrase, "go west, young man." As a philosophy, Manifest Destiny was often used to justify the removal of Native Americans from their land. As a white settler, Cashup was part of that. Yet he helped the tribes and maintained friendly relations.

Mary Ann told her family that she "always marveled at the Indian women because of their curiosity." They visited her occasionally and asked how she was able to grow such a robust garden. She showed them how to use manure to fertilize. This mutual interest, she said, helped to develop their relationship. Mary Ann and the family recognized that tribes had been living in the region for centuries and were not violent by nature. "But political leaders wanted to be protective of settlers," says Pat Mick, with some sarcasm. Mick is the great-granddaughter of Amy Charlotte Davis, Cashup's youngest daughter. She had heard these stories directly from Amy. It is one of the very few examples in which someone alive today can talk about conversations they had with one of Cashup's children. As Amy was Cashup's youngest daughter and lived into the 1960s, she is the primary witness of the family's pioneer experiences. Amy's daughter Mary Klein (Mick's grandmother) also recounted Amy's stories: "She says whites and Indians would've integrated peacefully if the troops had just let them be."

Later generations of Cashup and Mary Ann's family also held deep respect for Indians. As adults, the Davis children invited them into their homes for dinner and forged working relationships. Julia Davis Eckhart, the unofficial family historian, wrote about the experiences she had as a child in the home of her father Henry "Ed" Davis, one of Cashup's sons. She admits she was a little nervous as a young girl when the Indians came to dinner but, nevertheless, that exposure and demonstration of respect went far.

To be clear, this is not a story of a "white savior." We don't recount such episodes to say tribes were being saved by Cashup and his family. They weren't. We merely mean to say that in the context of a time of great tension and even war, Cashup's peaceful actions and beliefs were notable.

Many people wanted peace. Cashup did something about it.

SIX

THE STAGE STOP AND THE ADVENT OF "CASHUP"

"Now if there is any man in this, or any other country, [who] can extend a right royal welcome, it is Cash-up."

Spokane Falls Review

"DO YOU WANT TO OFFEND me?"

"Certainly not, Mr. Davis. I only want to know how much we owe you for our entertainment since yesterday afternoon."

"You don't owe me anything, Miss West."

That is the conversation recounted by Leoti L. West, a young girl who, in July 1880, with a friend stayed the night at James Davis's stage stop called "Steptoe Station." Years later, West became a newspaper columnist and wrote about that exchange. Several of her newspaper clippings were saved for generations in a Davis family scrapbook. The yellowed, scissor-sliced clipping gives a rare glimpse of James as he began to catapult into regional stardom as a popular proprietor of a dance hall, hotel, restaurant, and general store, anchored by a massive, spring-fed water trough and corral for tired horses driven by stagecoach drivers. The capacious ten-room farmhouse he built for his family after that abrupt trip took on double duty as the family's business headquarters, which was now in full launch.

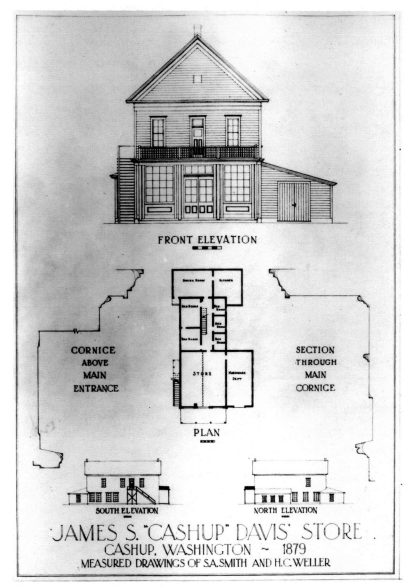

FRONT ELEVATION

CORNICE
ABOVE
MAIN
ENTRANCE

SECTION
THROUGH
MAIN
CORNICE

PLAN

SOUTH ELEVATION

NORTH ELEVATION

JAMES S. "CASHUP" DAVIS' STORE
CASHUP, WASHINGTON ~ 1879
MEASURED DRAWINGS OF S.A. SMITH AND H.C. WELLER

Blueprints for the stage stop that James "Cashup" Davis built, 1879.
From Washington State University Manuscripts, Archives, and Special
Collections, restored by Jim Martin.

The stage stop, opened in 1877 and expanded in 1879, made
him wealthier. And famous. James, the shrewd businessman
whenever he needed to purchase or sell goods, insisted on "cash

up front"—never owing, trading, or bartering, as was common practice. A newspaper account from the time said a Colfax storekeeper coined the nickname first: "There were a number of Davises living in Colfax at the time and several of them bore the names of James. One day while 'Cash-up' was making a purchase, a bystander asked the storekeeper how he distinguished the different Davises on his books. 'Oh,' replied the store-keeper, 'this Davis always pays cash up and there is no need of putting him on the books. From that day Davis was known as 'Cash-up' and it has stuck to him all through the intervening years and will follow him to his grave."

Dealing in cash allowed him to negotiate for the most advantageous price—to the point that it not only earned him respect but also some ill feelings from farmers and others who often needed to barter or borrow because they simply didn't have currency on hand. So unusual was his practice to use cash only that his reputation became known far and wide. The nickname made him a rare one-name celebrity. As we have referred to him as "James" from the outset of this book, we can finally call him by his better-known nickname, Cashup. Many folks get a nickname because they are liked or respected—sometimes both. The nickname Cashup is unique and distinguished. And in all my years, I have never heard of it handed out to anyone else.

"I'll give you $2.50, cash up." Cashup was fictionally quoted by Karl Allen who, among the many journalists reporting about the famous Davis, may have had access to the most reliable information. "In this manner of speech," wrote Allen, describing how Cashup did business, "with his characteristic give it or leave it alone air . . . Cold cash, in those days, was at a premium, and Davis was one of the few men who were in a position to demand closer prices by reason of their good fortune."

I chuckle when I recall the cash factor about Cashup because I, too, have a proclivity for cash. Not in a wallet or in a money clip.

Spokane Review article about James Davis, relating the story of how he received the nickname "Cashup." December 8, 1891. From *Spokesman-Review* archives.

Instead, I ingloriously wrap it with a rubber band. I have always preferred zero debt. Pay it off, sometimes with cash.

Journalists offered a variety of descriptors about Cashup in newspaper accounts: Big in personality while short in stature, charismatic, gregarious, intelligent, well spoken, politically engaged while somewhat religiously ambivalent, "a white-haired patriarch, but his heart was young," receding hair with a white, moderately cropped beard, deep-set eyes, prominent cheek bones, and exuberant energy. And James was always friendly—unless you got on his wrong side, in which case, he would not hesitate to snap at you. "The little old man—a fierce character," said Johnson. "He didn't give in to anybody. One man from Rosalia—they call him Hank Smith—and he said 'he was a boxy son of a bitch' but they admired him. Respected him."

In the late 1870s and early 1880s, Cashup's three adult children, who had remained in the Midwest, rejoined the family on the Palouse. In 1880, daughter Frances Davis McMeekin and her husband Andrew took the train out from Iowa with their six children. After arriving, they purchased railroad land to farm and earned additional money hauling grain from farms to Walla Walla or other shipping points. Eldest son William Davis and daughter Laura also came with families in tow. Letters from Cashup and Mary Ann suggest that family was extremely important to them and no doubt they were proud to have the entire clan living close by again. With Cashup's reputation and wealth expanding, it was a fortuitous time for the children to be near their parents.

Cashup's farming business boomed. The soil was fertile, yes, but Cashup was a darned fine farmer who embraced new ideas and technology. We know this about him from the following evidence: His family patented a more efficient thresher for harvest. He explained to a New York newspaper reporter how he maximized crops, knowing when to let a field rest versus turning a harvest. He planted orchard trees that would bear ripe fruit in stages rather than all at once. His yields were notably high and he made a lot of money from his farming. He was forward-thinking.

The Davis family helped build and launch a school nearby. It was likely located near the base of Steptoe Butte, a few hundred yards northeast of what is now Bethel Cemetery in the present-day town of Steptoe. Little was written about the schoolhouse. For many years, the school was known simply as "the Davis School" or "the Davis Schoolhouse."

Education thus must have been strongly valued by Cashup. Indeed, in what is probably the most well-known photo of him, he sits in his reading chair, clutching a book in his lap. Pioneers like Cashup were often ardently self-educated in physics, literature, history, and all manner of other topics, even though the topics may or may not have directly related to their lives. Typically, they learned for the sake of learning and consequently stockpiled books as they migrated west, handing them down to offspring. Cashup bequeathed his respect for education. My dad, Cashup's grandson, often said, "get a solid education; no one can ever take it away from you." I've followed his advice.

As new arrivals began to populate the Palouse, more and more travelers stopped at Cashup's place. One family, the large McCroskey clan, arrived on the Palouse in 1879 just a few years after Cashup and homesteaded adjacent to his place. Headed by Joshua Philander Theodore McCroskey and Mary Minerva Gallaher McCroskey, who had moved west from Tennessee, the family included eleven children. And, like the Davis family, all the McCroskey kids had been born before they pioneered westward. The McCroskey and the Davis families, in fact, became leaders of the Palouse. And the gaggle of children from both families grew up together. The paths of the McCroskeys and the Davises would intertwine many years later in fascinating and important ways.

The stage stop thrived. There are stories of all-night dances, lavish dinners in the dining room, a post office located inside, and stage-coach drivers eager to reach this ideally located and well-equipped stage stop on the way to or from Spokane Falls (which later became known solely as Spokane), a city quickly becoming the dominant urban area in the Inland Empire. Allen wrote that stagecoach drivers, along with ship captains and innkeepers, were among the "big men" of the old West, and many were household names. Among the drivers who regularly stopped at Cashup's Steptoe Station was Felix Warren, perhaps the most famous stagecoach driver of the era in the region. Felix's brother Joseph later became Seattle's police chief, and one of his lead drivers became a crucial employee of Cashup. Felix often drove the line from Walla Walla, Colfax, and Lewiston to Spokane and Fort Colville. When famed drivers like Felix Warren endorsed you, you became a household name as well. And notoriety meant money.

Cashup Davis' legendary stage stop midway between Spokane and Walla Walla in the Washington Territory, circa 1882. From Washington State University Manuscripts, Archives, and Special Collections.

A glowing account of the most well-known of a well-known group came from newspaperman Allen:

> The hotels or road houses and their proprietors, were better known to the early day travelers than the towns. Among the most popular of these was the Umatilla House at The Dalles, the St. Louis hotel at Walla Walla, the Raymond House at Lewiston, the Ewart House, operated by Captain and Mrs. James Ewart at Colfax, Gray's California House at Spokane Falls, and "Cashup's Inn" at Steptoe Station. "Wild Goose" Bill (William) Condon in the great bend of the Columbia River and Okanogan Smith, north of the Columbia, were well-known characters of the early days. But to Cashup Davis, most widely known of them all must go the credit for attracting the attention of the immigrants to the great Palouse country.

Julia Davis Eckhart adds in her family letters, "It was the favorite place for the young folks in all the upper country north of the Snake River."

A *Spokane Falls Review* reporter in 1883 noted that Cashup has "a fine general store, post office, blacksmith shop, a public hall in which at the last gathering of the stalwart sons and daughters no less than eighty couples participated in tripping the light fantastic," a very old phrase that means elated dancing.

Spokane's *Spokesman* newspaper reported: "Nearly every person knows, or has heard of 'Cash Up' Davis and not a single pioneer is without knowledge and acquaintance of their friend." The paper later reported that he was the "jolliest of hosts."

Pullman Herald editor Karl Allen wrote:

> Both the young and the old of the entire countryside, from Colfax to Spokane Falls, flocked to the dance hall to step the minuet, the polka, the quadrille and the waltz to the music furnished by Cashup's orchestra, known as the best in the new country, and composed of Cy and Andy Privett of Colfax.
>
> Cashup had a mania for company, and the bigger the crowd and the longer it stayed, the better his mood. On many a morning the strains of 'Privett Bros.' Stringed Orchestra' could still be heard above the shuffle of many pairs of feet when the less frivolous settlers were arising to begin their day's work. Each swain and every belle came at dusk, prepared to dance until daylight. On occasions, the merrymakers would find themselves snowed in, and would stay for days, or until the weather broke, Cashup the while playing his part as host right royally and making every minute of the prolonged festivities one of pleasure.

Indeed, so swept away by the music and merriment, Cashup himself would join in, playing his horn. "He could execute the sailor's hornpipe with many a nautical flourish and was past master in dancing the Virginia Reel, the Money Musk and all of the dances which were part of every program," Allen wrote.

Special parties, dances, or balls were held on Christmas and New Year's Eve, as evidenced in a January 15, 1885, letter sent from Gretta Swegle, a sixteen-year-old neighbor girl from a well-known pioneer family, to her sister Ida: "Prince, Goldie and I went to Cashup Davises to a ball Christmas Evening had a way up good time." Her letters tell of attending a dance that lasted "from dark 'til dawn and at which the guests were served oyster stew, free!" The Swegle family reports that, while the quote remains widely referenced, the letter itself is now lost. Oyster stew would have been quite rare for the Palouse. The oyster-filled saltwater barrels would have to have been hauled from the Pacific Ocean up the Columbia River more than 400 miles, and, if the rivers were running high, up the Snake River for a bit before the shipment transferred overland to wagons for the final 140 miles or so to Cashup's stage stop. Only then could the mollusks be found in the stew pots. Consequently, when served, the delicacy commonly made local headlines.

"Now if there is any man in this, or any other country, [who] can extend a right royal welcome, it is Cash-up," reported the *Spokane Falls Review* in 1883.

Firsthand stories were spreading, as reflected in this 1880 newspaper story:

> Soon after 7 o'clock we reached the hospitable domicile of Mr. Davis, and were heartily received by that gentleman and his family although we were not expected and the family was on the eve of retiring for the night. After we had removed our wraps . . . we were escorted by our host

to the hall and imagine our surprise at finding here the best and most comfortable dancing hall in the Palouse. The building is 60 x 30 feet and two stories high. The upper story is exclusively set apart for a hall and is provided with comfortable seats, and music stand, and is well lighted and heated.

Immediately on entering the hall, the Privett string band which accompanied us, struck up a waltz and the jolly company indulged in a delightful whirl which was followed in quick succession by various other dances for a period of two hours when supper was announced and we all repaired to the dining room and eagerly devoured the bountiful repast that was spread before us. Supper over, we returned to the hall and resumed dancing which was kept up until the small hours of the morning.

What's astonishing about this firsthand account is that Cashup and his family, as written, were not expecting these arrivals and were on their way to bed for the night. Yet, the unexpected guests not only brought the band with them but were also served a magnificent dinner.

Then, on August 12, 1882, Cashup's fame rose to a new level. Residents of the Palouse knew their local celebrity hit the big time when an article appeared in the *New York Evening Post*, written by a reporter identified only by initials "C. J. W." He profiled Cashup in a story that was reprinted in many newspapers for America to read. It read, in part: "No better fate can befall you at night than to find 'Cashup'; for that means comfort, luxury, pleasure galore, and, what is better than all, a man of sense and uprightness." He was a star; so much so that when Cashup visited a nearby town, his very presence made news and got people talking. A letter from Maida Harrison, written in 1968 when she was eighty-one, recollects a time when she was a very young girl

Cashup Davis and a woman—perhaps Mary Ann—can be seen standing on the balcony of his famous stagecoach stop as patrons gather outside, circa 1885. From the collection of Jim Martin.

and saw Cashup when he visited Colfax. "Every one was having a great to do [when] Cash Up Davis was in town. Of course, I was all eyes & ears. Finally, I saw him. A big crowd of men standing around talking. Some one said 'that is Cash Up Davis.'"

His renown having expanded, Cashup didn't disappoint his customers. When they settled up at the register at his stage stop, he made sure to exclaim "Cash Up!" to their great delight, according to a clipping from an unidentified newspaper in the family collection. Indeed, he quickly became the most prominent voice promoting the Palouse, specifically, the area around Steptoe Butte, as evidenced in a *Spokane Falls Review* story that ran on July 28, 1883:

"This, gentlemen," said Mr. Davis, "is to be Steptoe City. Here the railroad company have made their survey, and here I donate them land for depot, shops, etc. If not satisfied with the donation made, I shall give them more. Yonder you see two springs on that hill-side, where that grain is ripening; pipes can be laid from these springs and carry water to every house in town to the top story. Right here will be a park and fountain, and when in a few weeks this grain is removed the surveyors begin the work of platting what will be the most charming burg in Whitman county, Steptoe City."

His pronouncement is a little unclear. Steptoe City? At that time, there was Steptoe Butte, Steptoe Station, where Cashup's stage stop was located and, seven miles south, in 1875, the tiny hamlet of Steptoe had already been founded. Cashup was mightily promoting "Steptoe City" where he would donate some of his land to the railroad, suggesting he was referring not to the town of Steptoe to the south but to his Steptoe Station. You can almost hear Cashup speaking loudly, arms flailing, a crusader for development, his back arched in supreme confidence, maybe even standing on a box to dominate the gathered crowd of believing businessmen.

Cashup, always confident in his life, was now awash in adulation, success, and wealth—fueling his confidence even further. As more settlers arrived, the better Cashup's business prospered. And he was an incessant and credible promoter, always positive and always optimistic—even, occasionally, when he should not have been. Indeed, his irrepressible optimism would soon take him, quite literally, to the pinnacle project of his life—for better or worse. No, he did not seem to feel that his great success, wealth, and fame were enough. He seemed compelled to continue on with new endeavors, to achieve more, despite the risks.

Nearly lost in the historical record of Cashup Davis was one very telling conversation he had with O. N. Bell and Bell's father in winter of 1877. Bell and his father had just arrived on the Palouse on horseback and had stopped at Cashup's stage stop on their way to Spokane Falls to start new lives. The conversation occurred only weeks or months after Cashup had opened his successful stage stop. Bell writes in a pioneer reminiscence that Cashup urged him to homestead right there. Writes Bell: Cashup "told us the land was vacant for twenty-five miles around his place and insisted on my father locating a homestead there. He told us that he was going to build a wagon road up to the top of Steptoe butte, a hotel, dance hall and observatory." This private conversation, recounted by an elderly Bell in the *Colville Examiner* fifty-four years later, would provide a hint of Cashup's future and the future of the Palouse itself.

The true story of exactly when Cashup began planning his hotel can now be told: It was in 1877, according to Bell, before the full construction of his stage stop had even been completed.

And that hotel was next.

SEVEN

THE PALOUSE
BECOMES RENOWNED

Our water is pure, our climate health;
The soil is so rich, the farmers grow wealth.
On which, from year to year, the values rise,
So the first who come will prove to be wise.

ANONYMOUS POEM ABOUT THE PALOUSE FROM THE 1880S

CASHUP WOULD HAVE ENJOYED SEEING what happened to John Dixon on August 11, 2020. Dixon was on pace to shatter all the winter wheat harvest records in recorded American history. "He says, 'Dude, like, your math's wrong!'" recalled Dixon, an ebullient forty-six-year-old Palouse wheat farmer. He was operating his combine, trying to calculate the astonishing yield unfolding with third-party certifier Steve Van Vleet. And he had only a few acres left. But he still couldn't believe it. "Instantly, I'm thinking maybe my math is wrong!?"

It is ingrained in Dixon's memory: August 11 was a beautiful sunny day as he harvested the winter wheat crop on the land he farms near Pomeroy, in Garfield County, Washington, about forty miles southwest of Colfax. Clad in his usual short-sleeved shirt, blue jeans, and John Deere hat, he added, "pretty much the same thing every day." But this was no ordinary day.

The wheat kept pouring into the bulk tank and then on into the bank-out wagon before hitting the trucks. The two continually double-checked their calculations. As their onboard computers churned out real-time data, they became as excited as a couple of kids at Christmas. A typical yield for American wheat farmers usually falls far short of one hundred bushels per acre. On the Palouse, 100 is normal for winter wheat, with 125 bushels not uncommon. But this year was different. Dixon knew that news of his impending record had gotten out and people were just starting to show up to see if he would make history.

His bulk tank normally never filled up at this point in the harvest. But then Dixon saw Van Vleet outside the cabin, waving his hands, indicating that "it's full!" That's the moment he knew. Immediately he thought to himself, "Oh my Lord."

The yield was 189.986 bushels per acre, farmwide—not just a freak acre here or there. All told, the farm produced almost 190 bushels of winter wheat per acre.

"It's crazy!" Dixon exclaimed. He and his family have farmed on the Palouse for generations. Dixon's father worked for a man named Alex McGregor and, as a nineteen-year-old, John Dixon had also farmed for McGregor, who taught him a lot. Indeed, McGregor knows this Palouse soil as well as anyone ever has. His family arrived here in 1882 from Scotland, after many farmers there were forced off their farms by the Enclosure Movement, which changed land ownership from a commons arrangement (village-held lands) into a private one (owned by an individual).

McGregor says his ancestors, who were no doubt acquainted with Cashup, were "crusty old Scottish sheep herders [who] ended up with a lot of ground." Four or five generations later, Alex continued the family tradition of farming and ranching, but added to his credentials by earning a PhD, becoming a college professor, writing history books, and starting The McGregor Company, dedicated to helping farmers increase yields wisely

Wheat harvest on the Palouse, 2020. A video frame from the Cashup Davis documentary.

using fertilizers and other strategies. McGregor also served as the president of the Washington Association of Wheat Growers and remains a leader in Palouse agriculture.

McGregor was there in the field that day to watch his young friend break the record. He was mighty proud. "We get three-quarters of our moisture during the wintertime and early spring so winter wheat gets more water," McGregor says. It is ideal especially for winter wheat because the loess soils have perfect moisture retention. "In most places, if you don't get rainfall regularly every two to three weeks, your crop suffers. But here, because of the soils, in part, and the Mediterranean climate we share on [the] Pacific Coast," yields are consistently the best in North America. Indeed, the rainfall during that record-setting growing season was 16 inches in places.

Rich Koenig also appreciates the quality of soil. He bends his lanky six-foot frame to kneel on the soil near the top of a Palouse rolling hill—one of thousands—as the sun drops lower toward the horizon in the cloudless blue sky. A truck loaded to the brim with newly harvested wheat rumbles along a winding country road far below, its engine muffled by the distance. Picking up a handful of dirt, Rich shuffles it in his hand and lets it scatter slowly back to the ground. A faint summer breeze carries some of it away.

"The Palouse soil really is that good," he says.

Koenig is not a farmer or a chamber of commerce type promoting all things local. He is not even a Palouse native. He is a quiet guy, a widely recognized soil scientist at nearby Washington State University, whose agricultural science department is respected worldwide. And he recently served as the interim dean of the university's college of agricultural, human, and natural resource sciences. What's his take on all the hype surrounding the fertility of the Palouse soil?

"It is true! Yep. It is true. You don't find soils like this anywhere else in the world." He explains exactly what makes the soil so valuable—the loess or fine soil that is a windblown mixture of silt, sand, and clay. When the ice dams broke near the end of the last ice age, the massive floods brought silt that was subsequently blown across the region, forming the rolling hills of the Palouse. The loess, a dune topography, Koenig says, accumulated as far as the eye can see.

But it turns out the soil isn't the only thing that's remarkable about the Palouse. The region's Mediterranean climate means that most of the moisture arrives as snow and rain in the winter, when it is needed most, and less so in summer, when it would harm standing stalks and delay harvest.

The final secret ingredient is sometimes overlooked yet has been underway for thousands of years. Koenig notes that the thick bunchgrass, sometimes waist high, adds precious nutrients to the soil. All of these features create and have been creating perfect nutrient-rich soil. At a perfect soil depth. With perfect timing from seasonal rain and sunshine, leading to perfect water retention. The Perfect Palouse.

Is the benchmark 200 bushels per acre not far away? It would be the Holy Grail of wheat farming.

"We're getting pretty close to it," says McGregor.

Dixon says Van Vleet told him they might hit 200 that day, often reminding him that "'Oh!' We're not that far from 200!'" Hoping that the outbursts wouldn't jinx it, Dixon admitted, "I kept my mouth shut."

There is one place in the world that has a consistently higher wheat yield than the Palouse: a small area in the northern part of Great Britain and Scotland where they receive a lot more moisture. Nevertheless, experts from that area and from all over the world come to the Palouse to see how farmers here produce such consistently high yields. When they arrive in the area, they can't miss the road signs posted around the Palouse that say, "Entering Whitman County, the nation's leading wheat-producing county." Palouse farmers have had bragging rights ever since Cashup and his fellow pioneers first turned dirt in the 1870s and started telling everyone back East to get out to the Palouse before the land was all taken.

Keep in mind that high yields on the Palouse were every bit as impressive prior to modern fertilizers and technology. Cashup told the *New York Evening News* in August 1882 that their wheat yields were 40–45 bushels per acre. In July the next year, he told the *Spokane Falls Review* the same thing—and the reporter confirmed it himself. The claim seemed so outrageous that members of Congress sent out United States Department of Agriculture soil expert Thomas W. Simons to investigate the craziness. "He wrote of a huge crop of grain without a drop of moisture from seed to harvest—which was stretching it a bit," concedes McGregor, who wrote about Simons in his book, *Counting Sheep: From Open Range to Agribusiness on the Columbia Plateau*. But Simons's visit made the claims official.

Now, let it be known that the size of your yield is sort of like the size of the fish that got away. Trust, but verify. "Nobody was hitting forty-five bushels per acre," says a skeptical Frank Hager, who turned one hundred years old in 2020 and grew up on the farms of the Palouse. His parents and grandparents told him all about Cashup Davis and the grandiose claims that sometimes came from exuberant promoters. Hager remembers when wheat prices crashed in 1929. He says "twenty-five bushels per acre, you did pretty well. If you said you did more than that, nobody believed [you]."

"A vast expanse" of fertile prairie, wrote newspaperman Allen in 1919, "now places Whitman county in the front rank of cereal producing counties of the world."

Returning to the 1880s: Quick landgrabs by newcomers benefiting from the Homestead Act or by those able to purchase land from others occurred, the latter especially from the railroad companies that had been granted much of the American West by the federal government in exchange for developing transportation networks. Other settlers added to their existing acreage. As a result, farmers were growing wheat, oats, barley, fruit trees, and other crops at yields that America had rarely seen. Even potatoes were raising eyebrows. Cashup bragged to his sons that they were growing "the best-tasting potatoes you've ever had."

When the *New York Evening Post* ran a feature on Cashup in 1882, the reporter chronicled a rare "conversation" with Cashup. In reading the profile included below, remember that reporters in this era had no recorders. Handwritten notes often don't transcribe a conversation perfectly, even when a writer uses shorthand notation. Still, the piece gives a rare glimpse into the farming life of Cashup and the Palouse in those early days.

Correspondence of the *New York Evening Post* (1882)

It is a question how much wheat to the acre farming in this locality would obtain if they would till the land in the same thorough way we are accustomed to [back] East. Mr.

Davis, for instance, has simply plowed his land once, and then sowed it without more preparation.

"Don't you backset?" I asked him.

"Not at all; just plow and then drag it in. In Ohio, Wisconsin and Iowa, where during my life I have farmed, my custom was to plow deep in June, let the sod rot and lie over until spring, then harrow the seed in."

"Then one great saving is that of time."

"Yes, in this way. The sod there had to lie a year and rot. Here we can plow and put in wheat immediately. I have plowed the clean prairie the first week in May, and having no threshing machine, I tramped it out with horses and got forty-five bushels to the acre. There was a good deal of waste. I think a machine would have given me three to five bushels more per acre off that piece."

"Do you approve of such superficial farming?"

"Well, I used to be very slow-going when I first came here, and never would take such liberties with the land. Take, for instance, that wheat just referred to. The fact is, I never intended to cut that wheat when I sowed it. I knew it would make good feed, and I kept plowing and sowing until I had down to wheat and oats forty-five acres. I intended to cut it green and use it in the stack for fodder during the winter. I had about fifty or sixty head of horses and seventy to eighty head of cattle at that time. But when the grain came up it gained so and looked so well that I had to cut it to see what it would yield; and, as I say, there was forty-five wheat and sixty oats to the acre. Since then, on a field over yonder I sold to James Tannatt, I have raised seventy-five bushels. Now I am as shiftless as any of 'em."

"Well, do you approve of this method of farming?"

"No, indeed; I would rather do thorough work and get a third more yield at least."

"How much land have you now?"

"A section—640 acres."

"When did you come into possession of it?"

"I bought it about two years ago. I had been occupying it for four years before that."

"How much have you under cultivation?"

"I have 150 acres of wheat, about the same of oats, and the rest is barley."

"There must be some drawbacks and discouragements everywhere. Will you mention what you have found them to be?"

"Well, let me see," musingly, and trying to think, "why, right here, where I am, wood is scarce, but there is the best of cedar, fir, pine and tamarack twenty miles away. It is on government land. I can have it for the hauling."

Mr. Davis I find to be more optimistic than some others on this point. The fact is that the nearest forests are twenty miles away. Lumber is high and wood a valuable commodity. Coal sells at $17.50 per ton. The farmers make light in more senses than one of this, not seeming to heed it in their calculations of profits. The fact is the winters are far from severe. Mr. Davis said, in answer to a question of mine on this point:

"Sometimes there will come a little shake of snow, five or ten inches, and then a Chinook wind will melt it, and the air is quite warm. The grass that has mattered on the land supports horses all winter. I have never seen the temperature lower than seven degrees below zero."

"Can you not mention something more discouraging to settlers?"

"Well," after a pause, "no. Everything's been so prosperous with me and with those I have seen that I can't find any fault with it. There has never been a sign of failure of wheat, oats or barley since I have been here. Men that worked for me at seventy-five cents to a dollar a day are now worth several thousand dollars."

THE NECESSARY CAPITAL.

"How much capital do you think is required for a man to start in successfully?"

"It's hard to get at. But let's see; 160 acres is a farm big enough on this prairie. I suppose a man could buy that much land at $4. That would be $640. Then he would need to visit one of the saw mills (there are four within ten miles of here,) and would find that he could put up a plain frame one-story-and-a-half house, if he will help himself, for $300. Then he would need a plough, $22; a harrow $22; a wagon, $145; and a team, which will cost $150, making about $340. He could dig a well in two or three days himself. Household necessaries and clothing are very cheap here. Then, if he hires his breaking done, which is what I should do, say fifty acres the first year, would cost him $2.75 per acre, and the laborer finds his own team, etc. He can get plenty of men at that. Then he takes his own team and harrows the land; then sows and drags it in. Now he has time to fix up his house, and build his barn, and get stock yard for threshing, etc. When it is time to thresh— supposing the forty was sown in April along in August, our friend can have his grain cut and threshed out, say twenty acres easy, every day, ready for marketing, for it's a quick job; head the wheat right into the thresher, and it is ready for the market at a cost of $1 per acre for threshing. I will agree to take up a quarter section in this country anywhere, and agree to pay for it the first year, and have nothing to do after I am started a good share of the time. Why, my land has supported my large family, paid for all improvements you can see those barns over yonder, etc., and paid for itself three times over."

"One question more; Why do I find cultivation spread mostly over the lowlands?"

"Because they are easiest handled, and appear to be, from the experience further east in Montana, more fertile. But the highest lands are the best. I will raise the finest wheat in the country on Old Steptoe Bluff itself, or my name is not J. S. Davis."

C. J. W.

As the reporter suspected, Cashup did not divulge some of the natural hardships that beset him and the other Palouse pioneers. The Palouse, like many areas of the great American West, was not always hospitable and required toughness and hard work to survive.

Deadly Winters

Cashup told the *Post* that he had never seen the winter temperature drop to more than minus seven degrees. But some years were bad. Really bad. For example, the winter of 1889–90 was a killer. The snow, temperatures, and wind conspired to kill livestock and horses that were huddling up against fences in a desperate attempt to stay alive. These were "huge losses," says McGregor.

After a stretch of winter weather, warmer temperatures tricked pioneers into thinking an early spring was arriving. But the killer weather loomed just around the corner, according to a county history. "The first flurry came on the night of December 15, covering the ground to a depth of several inches. Succeeding falls came at intervals until by January 15th the ground had upon it a blanket of snow about two feet thick." Trains and other travel were shut down for two weeks or so, which was not entirely unusual. "Spring-like weather succeeded. The snow quickly melted and for about three weeks the winter was mild as could be desired," according to the account. "Then came a sudden change. There was another heavy snowfall, accompanied by wind and cold. Many of the largest stock owners were entirely out of feed and unable to secure any. The thermometer fell as low as twenty-one degrees below zero, reaching its lowest point February 25th. The much-wished-for chinook so long delayed its coming that hundreds of cattle perished . . . and resulted most disastrously for stock men."

Julia Davis Eckart wrote about her father Ed's battle with killer winters. She did not mention the year but it could very well have been that same fateful winter of 1889–90. "One year my father had sixty head of horses in the Big Bend country for winter pasture. He kept a man with them until he thought all danger of storms were over. Then he brought the man home and left the horses there, with the snow gone and plenty of green pasture. This was in March. After that time in the Big Bend there came a blinding snowstorm. Drove the horses as far as they could go, up against the fences of course. The snow covered all the green feed and there the poor horses died of hunger. They said some of the manes and tails were eaten off the horses."

Under the snow and ice and wind that winter, crops lay quiet and largely unaffected. Only a portion of the economy was hit.

Invasion of the Coulee Crickets

Then there were the crickets, invasive and overwhelming. These were "armies" of coulee crickets (*Peranabrus scabricollis*), which can swarm and clean out every speck of green vegetation across more than one hundred square miles. The earliest account of a cricket invasion in the area was 1873, according to a comprehensive report sent to Washington Gov. Ernest Lister in 1918, just as Cashup and his family had arrived on the Palouse.

More invasions came, including a particularly bad one that started in 1892 and continued for ten years straight. But the 1903 infestation was "the most disastrous cricket devastation the state has ever known," noted the governor's report. Newspapers from that fateful ten-year period provided frequent news coverage. Reports used the term "grasshopper" interchangeably with "crickets," even though they refer to two distinct insects: grasshoppers have smaller antennae and make noise rubbing their legs with their wings, while crickets rub their legs together. In swarms, both species devastate crops. "Grasshoppers have got in their deadly work on several hundred acres of wheat near Colton," said the *Pullman Herald* on August 10, 1895; and the next year on August 22, "During the heat of the day, when the wind is from the cast, the air is full of grass-hoppers." "The adult female lays her eggs," said another, "from around July 15th on, each female laying about 70 eggs at a time and repeating this process several times, providing the weather remains favorable." It continued: "The eggs winter over and hatch during the first few warm days of the spring. It is at this time that control measures are most effective."

The only control measures in the earliest days available involved simply recruiting every person possible to help dig ditches or holes and the use of boards and makeshift fencing— "cricket fences," they were called—to herd the crickets into the ditches and light them on fire.

"My father [Cashup's son Ed] with other pioneers," Julia Davis Ekhart wrote, "plowed ditches around his crops, drove the crickets into the ditches as best they could[;] after the crickets fell into the ditches they couldn't get out, then the farmers burned them with straw. They had to be gathered every morning, but this got them."

One year in particular, after the founding of nearby Washington State College (later University) in 1890, McGregor says that the cricket invasion was so bad that farmers recruited agriculture researchers and scientists to help build a trench seven miles long. "This menace affects all the farming districts of Eastern Washington," said the report to the governor. So desperate were farmers to counter the cricket invasion, they employed poison. As the types of livestock expanded and diversified in the region, farmers even tried to recruit the animals into the war on crickets. "Four hundred hogs were brought into the district and herded on these crickets, destroying thousands of them, . . . incidentally making the hogs sick. Turkeys and chickens were also experimented with, but the construction of the cricket is such that neither hogs, chickens, nor turkeys can feed on them to advantage until after the crickets have been burned or singed. In that condition they make very desirable stock feed for poultry and probably for hogs." "Indians and white men vouch for this report," the report proclaims.

One account in neighboring Grant County said in 1918 that the federal government sent in an entomologist named Alfred C. Burrill to help fight the infestations like a military general: "Under Mr. Burrill's direction, all available help in the community was employed chiefly in building cricket fences and using torches. During the two months of April and May a hundred people were used, averaging a force of sixteen persons continuously for sixty days. During this time six distinct armies of crickets were encountered, moving as persistently in their different directions as an army of soldiers. These were all successfully conquered. It is reported that one army made six successive charges against different portions of a four-mile defense line."

One farmer reported: "This year twenty-four potato sacks were filled, with the burned or singed bodies of crickets and taken home by different workers and fed to their poultry. These sacks were estimated to contain over one million crickets, and they did not represent half the number that were believed to have been killed."

Ruinous Rain

The precious rain that fuels the crops can also kill them when it deluges fields before harvest, as it did in 1893. McGregor says it began raining that year before harvest and just kept on, "so that the crop was eventually ruined and of no value." The same ruinous rain that year was chronicled in a reminiscence letter written by Julia Eckart Davis years later: "was a rainy fall, rained so much causing most everyone to lose their crops. This was a year never to be forgotten by the pioneers." Lyman and Martha (Swegle) Curtis had come from Wisconsin to farm near Thornton. Lyman lost his entire wheat crop in the rains of '93, as well as his entire farm. Like many farmers, they leveraged the value of their land against a loan to purchase supplies to keep operating. That year, Curtis's bank or insurance company took it all back. It is a story that still resonates through the Curtis family descendants who still farm the land near there. "If you didn't make your payments," says Al Curtis, Lyman's great-grandson, "you were done." Al's sister Joanne Gfeller recalls, "it was something that was happening to every farmer around. . . . they were just trying to find a better life for their families." After the disaster, Lyman's sons built a feed storage building in Thornton and put their dad in charge of it. Stories of the rains of '93 are shared to this day.

Despite these periodic challenges from the natural world, Palouse farmers thrived during this time. Indeed, the historical record supports the kind of optimistic portrayal of wealth and prosperity on the Palouse that Cashup offered in his storytelling over the years. In short, there truly was money to be made. The year 1897 may go down as one of the best in that era, according to *An Illustrated History of Whitman County, Washington*. The weather was "exceptionally favorable" all year, "resulting in an exceptionally heavy yield." Global grain harvests had crashed in many places, so prices rose.

So large was the yield of wheat that fall that great difficulty was experienced in securing enough threshers to handle the grain. Harvest hands, too, were relatively scarce, and for a time it was feared that the husbandmen would lose part of their wealth from sheer inability to care for it. Warehouses were entirely inadequate to the demands upon them, and temporary structures had to be erected to shelter the surplus wheat. Prices continued high. Many farmers were enabled to remove large mortgages with the profits of that single crop, and the wheels of progress were everywhere set in motion. The clouds of financial distress were completely dispelled, and prosperity shone forth in its meridian strength and glory.

In 1896, the Whitman County assessor reported statistics to the state that suggested the county was moving beyond the rudimentary pioneer era:

- Farms in county: 4,668
- Acres in cultivation: 421,653
- Acres irrigated: 433
- Miles of irrigating ditches and canals: 9
- Number of fruit growers: 130
- Pounds of wool produced: 213,700
- Money invested in machinery and tools: $162,689
- Money invested in buildings: $5,705,044
- Creameries: 3
- Pounds of butter made during the year at home and in creameries: 114,912
- Men employed in farm work: 1,465
  - Average wages: $22.18 per month
- Men in clerical positions: 219
  - Average wages per month: $52

1896 Crop Yields in Whitman County

CROP	ACRES	YIELD PER ACRE	TOTAL COUNTYWIDE
Wheat	185,883	20 1/4 bushels	3,764,130 bushels
Oats	27,179	37 1/6 bushels	194,783 bushels
Barley	18,103	35 1/10 bushels	635,415 bushels
Rye	1,517	24 2/9 bushels	36,745 bushels
Corn	1,380 ¼	16 bushels	22,084 pounds
Hay	24,561	1 5/8 tons	39,911 tons
Sugar beets	17	16,000 pounds	272,000 pounds
Flax	1,516	11 3/4 bushels	17,813 bushels
Potatoes	1,588	99 7/8 bushels	150,901 bushels
Vegetables	1,777		
Fruit	2,973	$58 value	
Grapes	33		
Small Fruits	160		

From the top of Steptoe Butte, you can see farms all the way to the horizon in every direction. It can make you wonder about the economic value of all that rich farmland. So, Koenig did more than wonder. He and his academic team examined the historical records of all the farms in a fifty-mile radius of the butte and here is what he found, listed in dollar value from the year captured:

Eastern Washington Farm Revenues over 120-Year Span

YEAR	LIVESTOCK	CROPS	TOTAL
1900	$6,824,593 (39%)	$10,617,345 (61%)	$17,441,938
1960	$21,268,282 (22%)	$76,871,105 (78%)	$98,139,387
2020	$65,407,583 (10%)	$606,024,167 (90%)	$671,431,750

Koenig et al. 2020.

His results show an impressive agriculture economy all within view of the summit of Steptoe Butte, the center of the Palouse. It also showed how farmers over time came to recognize the yield of crops versus livestock; the percentage of the land area dedicated to crops in 1900 was 61% but grew to 90% by 2020.

***

"I always taste every apple," says David Benscoter as he takes a bite of a slightly unripe green one that elicits an oddly loud crunch. He chomps. Tastes. Not saying a word yet. Thinks. Chews. His face says it's not ripe yet.

"That has definitely a few weeks to go!" Laughter breaks out.

The bite comes from a Blue Pearmain apple picked from a 150-year-old tree planted by Cashup Davis and his family on the slope of Steptoe Butte. These are Cashup's apples. Benscoter founded the Lost Apple Project to locate apple varieties thought to be extinct. He's a former federal investigator who is now an "apple detective." He points to the next tree over: an Arkansas Beauty, a variety thought to be extinct until Benscoter investigated and had the apple tested in a lab. He has rediscovered numerous "lost apples" in his search over the past decade in the Northwest.

If you look closely, hidden under 150 years of shrubs and vegetation, there it is: An orchard. Still growing, still producing apples to this day. Damn good ones, too. Cashup's "special varieties" of apples were very well known throughout the Palouse, so much so that Theodore Smith, proprietor of the Palouse Nursery two miles east of Colfax, bought apple trees from Cashup and then sold them at his nursery. An advertisement in the *Colfax Gazette* in 1890 declares: "The only collection of hardy trees that have been proven in the Palouse country . . . Cashup Davis, ever ready to show you wonders from Steptoe Butte says: 'My trees are the only ones . . . that were worth a _____ [the ad literally left a blank space]. The rest have become black hearted.'" The price he charged for one hundred trees—enough to create a large orchard: $15.

"This was an orchard very similar to the way homesteaders planted, which was you planted early apples, you planted fall apples—the whole orchard, there are very few trees that are duplicates," Benscoter says. "Winter apples they could put in their cellar, [and] they [w]ould keep until next spring."

Cashup's trees were so well placed in the ravines to keep constant moisture flowing to them that, all these years later, they still produce beautiful apples. Roberts Burns, a competitor of Cashup's back then, also planted apple trees around the base of Steptoe Butte that still churn out the apples today. And, as we will see, Burns may have turned out to be much more than a mere competitor.

Benscoter says the apples "were such an important part of the history of this region."

And buried in the grass right there in Cashup's orchard ravine is an old stone step. It is not a random rock; it had been placed there by a human hand. Perhaps by Cashup himself, after stepping around his trees.

Food also came from the wild. The Palouse still had plenty of game to shoot, as described by Roberts: "He [Cashup] was a crack shot and all his boys became veritable nimrods for game, including deer, bear and elk, abounded in the nearby foothills and prairie chickens, grouse and pheasants were innumerable everywhere." Roberts goes even further, describing a trait in Cashup that would become exceedingly important and perhaps even saved his life: kindness. "Every domestic animal[,] including chickens and other poultry, was petted and named and not unusually coyotes, deer and bear were at home in the house enclosure of the barnyard, thoroughly tractable from kind treatment. In such an atmosphere, the spirit of comraderie [sic] pervaded the Davis family."

The Palouse was full of challenges that could ruin hopes. But it was also full of potential that could bring the pioneers great riches. And sometimes they were one and the same. Cashup was about to be smacked right between the eyes with one of the biggest changes the Palouse had ever seen, a change full of both profits and problems.

EIGHT

THE HOTEL ON THE HILL

Whether you think you can or you think you can't, you're right.

HENRY FORD

THE ADVERTISEMENT APPEARED IN THE *Colfax Gazette* on September 26, 1884:

Incredibly, Cashup Davis was announcing he, the person whose nickname was an homage to his preference for cash rather than credit, was willing to settle up with his customers for half in cash and half in IOUs. Moreover, he was also selling the merchandise on his shelves for what he paid for it, in exchange for someone willing to rent his store.

He was going out of business.

Davis was telling the entire Palouse he was hoping to put his legendary stage stop into someone else's hands. Why? Just as in the twentieth century when the automobile killed the blacksmith, in the 1880s, throughout the West, trains killed the stagecoach—and, with it, the stage stops. Railroad lines were being built incrementally and with steady certainty. Julia Davis Eckhart wrote, "The year 1880 saw the Northern Pacific railway building west from Fargo, North Dakota and east from the mouth of the Snake River and September 18, 1883 the last spike was driven at Gold Creek, Montana. The O. W. R. & N. Railroad [Oregon-Washington Railroad and Navigation] built a track from Palouse Junction on the Northern Pacific railroad to Colfax, WA and in 1886 the Spokane and Palouse Railroad finished its road as far as Oakesdale and Belmont, Washington from Spokane." Horses or horse-drawn wagons would still move people from one end of town to the other or to the next town over. But, for most intermediate and long-distance hauling of people and goods, the era of the horse-drawn wagon or stagecoach on the Palouse was done.

"The demand for big freight teams was over," wrote George McCroskey who, as the son of Cashup's neighbor J. P. T. McCroskey, knew Cashup well. "The old and battered stage coach passed over the old territorial road for the last time that year, and Cashup, noted far and near over the Northwest, settled down to the regime of an ordinary farm home."

It wasn't just Cashup, of course. Everyone who relied on the constant stream of stage traffic was doomed. McCroskey wrote,

"Sad days befell Cashup and the other stage station operators on the territorial road. That was in 1883 when the Northern Pacific began to operate its trains across the territory. The stage coaches dropped fewer and fewer passengers at Cashup's door and fewer and fewer freight teams stopped to drink at the 'biggest watering trough in the upper country.'"

Cashup may have seen the end coming when he had brashly announced earlier to a reporter that, in exchange for locating a new train station, he was willing to sell to the railroad all the land it needed in and around what he was calling "Steptoe City," hoping to harness the very weapon that was putting him out of business to help him build a city that he could lead to growth and prosperity through his irresistible positivity.

But—hold on. That pronouncement about Cashup retiring? To become an "ordinary" farmer?

Not a chance. Not Cashup Davis.

Rather than cry in his milk, he pondered, "What's next?" He was not done yet. He had something up his sleeve, something that had been brewing for a long time, years maybe, perhaps a lifetime. And now, in the midst of failure, he was ready to pivot. When most people might have abandoned hope after calamitous failure or just faded away, Cashup must have told himself, "I'll prove to the world this failure was out of my control, and I will now attempt my greatest achievement ever. Just watch."

He liquidated his stage stop, taking half in cash and half in IOUs, to settle his outstanding balances with customers at the very same time he was preparing to finance something much more ambitious—in fact, one of the biggest things the Palouse had ever seen. Cashup was going to build a grand, elaborate hotel right on top of Steptoe Butte. The view from the summit alone would draw people by the thousands. The quality of the establishment, the entertainment, and the food would be unsurpassed. With his vision, his following, his taste, his engineering prowess, his determination, his marketing, and his enthusiasm steering him, nothing would stop him in realizing his dream.

McCroskey put it this way: "He turned his attention to making a resort of Steptoe butte, a mountain with an unobstructed view, made by the Almighty it would seem, for a special purpose; a panorama not exceeded in the world; a lighthouse in eastern Washington and northern Idaho like one on the seashore to warn the mariner of danger and guide him along the way home; a guide post in the pioneer days to travelers lost many miles from home in the hills or on the plains, known long ago as the 'Silent Sentinel of the Palouse.'"

Conflicting accounts exist regarding how and when Cashup came to this grand vision. In an overly romantic newspaper account, one reporter wrote that "Cashup was ever the dreamer. And one day while contemplating his melancholy future he gazed upon the barren peak of Steptoe to became [sic] electrified with the idea of buying the mountain and erecting a hotel on its top." In this flowery account, you can almost hear the chorus singing and the camera panning upward. However, the historical record strongly suggests that Cashup's vision was not a sudden inspiration. Indeed, Cashup had been thinking of building a grand hotel atop the butte for years. Almost a decade prior, during an overnight stay at the stage stop in the winter of 1876, O. N. Bell and his father had heard Cashup's plan: "He told us that he was going to build a wagon road up to the top of Steptoe butte, [plus] a hotel, dance hall and observatory." Surely the conversation with Bell was not the first time Cashup had thought of this venture. You must understand that Steptoe Butte is so prominent, so strong, so omnipresent, one can't help but contemplate its presence. It would be consistent with the human condition to conclude that he had thought about building something on the top of the butte during those solitary days and nights during his first visit to the Palouse in 1872.

One could also assume that Cashup was harkening back to his childhood in England, where castles perched atop the hills around his hometown and just about everywhere else he traveled. The concept of a building overlooking the landscape was thus very familiar to him. The inspiration was in his blood. Many would call this hotel his "castle."

Now he had to get to work. He had to raise the money to buy the butte. He had to design this lavish hotel. He had to find the lumber and build a road up that monstrously steep hill. After hiring a contractor and workers to construct the hotel, he'd need to find unparalleled interior furnishings and décor, and create a restaurant that would offer the finest food and entertainment in the region. He had to figure out how to get fresh water to the summit. And he had to conjure some sort of attraction that would make visiting his hotel an absolute must.

On the day he advertised to liquidate to raise money, he was a year and a few days from turning seventy years old. Yet he was ready to invest his life savings on the new scheme. In fact, building a hotel of that stature would likely take long enough that Cashup would be seventy-two years old before it opened for business. In the pioneer era, the average life span was shorter than what it is today. And seventy-two-year-old men were often worn and tired after a hard life. But not Cashup.

No record exists of a conversation about this plan with his wife, Mary Ann. But such a conversation must have been, shall we say, animated. She had previously put her foot down in the middle of their journey to stop his plan to move to British Columbia. And her decision had been quite fortunate. This time, would she impede him yet again? We'll never know. My guess is she tried and failed. He was stubborn!

The 1888 US Census suggests that Cashup may have had some available help. It indicates that two sons and two daughters were living at home, along with Mary Ann, who, like Cashup, was

A surrey pulled by two horses pauses near Steptoe Butte, where Cashup's hotel can just be seen at the top of the hill, circa 1890. This rare photo shows the daunting task of climbing the butte to reach the hotel. From the collection of Jim Martin.

getting older but, at sixty-one, was still physically strong. Clarence, Mary Anne, Amy Charlotte, and Charley were all young and strong. But let's be clear: while no letters or direct quotes can be found, Cashup's family was not happy about his plans to spend the family's money on a hotel way up on the summit. So it is unclear how much help they provided.

The historical record is full of accounts that just about everyone told him he was crazy to do this. And maybe he was. "Well, he was determined to a fault," Randall Johnson told me. "When he got the notion of building that hotel, everyone in the territory thought that he was absolutely insane." Maybe for a person who sets his or her sights on something so lofty, so audacious, being a little crazy is to be expected. Listening to one's gut instinct and ignoring naysayers, as well as, at times, rational facts, can often give someone the drive to do what others can only imagine is impossible or even foolhardy.

Edith Erickson, the late Colfax historian and descendant of pioneers, wrote in *Colfax 100 Plus*, "The building of the hotel was a gigantic undertaking."

"Risk and reward" was a recurring theme throughout Cashup's life. And this endeavor was perhaps the biggest risk of all, an audacious idea that began in his heart, deepened in his head, and ultimately found expression via his and others' hands.

Buying the Butte

Once he raised the funds, he started spending it. He bought the top half or so of the butte from the O. W. R. & N. Company. The butte was part of the land that had been granted to them by the federal government to develop transportation networks in the West. The grant included miles of land on either side of the potential path of the railroad lines. And Cashup knew—and probably reminded them—that their land on the slopes of the butte was useless for trains. They certainly could not build a railroad track over the top of the massive butte. Cashup being Cashup, he quietly negotiated the purchase of 300 acres.

Cashup may have been known as a "homesteader." But, in fact, there is no record of him taking ownership of land through that process. The Homestead Act required a person to file a claim, improve the land, and remain on it for at least five years. He did not do that in St. John and did not do that on and near Steptoe Butte. Instead, he acquired some land through an alternate process called the Timber Culture Act, which helped him to become one of the biggest landowners in the region.

After all this, the crucial first step, buying the butte, was accomplished.

A rare illustration of Cashup's hotel on Steptoe Butte, from the *Spokesman-Review*, May 8, 1892. From the *Spokesman-Review* archives.

Design

The skills he had developed as a young man, leading a team of sixty men to build portions of the Dover Tunnel all those years ago, now came in very handy. He had also learned to dig wells while living in the Midwest. He had built a ten-room home in St. John and another ten-room home with several other buildings at his stage stop. His father had been a builder and lumberman. Cashup figured out how to hoist the massive beams and struts strong enough to withstand brutal windstorms at the summit.

Cashup wanted his hotel to astound visitors so they would keep coming back and bring more people with them. He designed it to be three stories high, 66 feet by 66 feet initially, with hotel rooms, a ballroom, a restaurant, a store, a stage, a parlor, and facilities to care for the horses that would bring visitors up the hill. He intended the hotel's interior to be so ornate and lavish that he hired a professional decorator: "I. B. Doolittle leaves today for Steptoe butte where he will paper and decorate the interior of Cashup's Hotel at the summit," announced the Whitman County *Gazette*.

Second step, design, accomplished.

Lumber

The Palouse features rolling hills and prairie. No forest. Cashup had told the *New York Evening Post* that "the nearest forests are twenty miles away. Lumber is high [priced] and wood a valuable commodity." Sawmills were still a new and rare industry on the Palouse in 1887. The historical record is conflicted regarding where Cashup got his lumber. Cashup's hotel would arguably need more lumber than almost anything ever constructed on the Palouse at that time. There were several possibilities: For about four years, a sawmill, built by Daniel Truax and his brother, had been in use in Tekoa (then called "Fork in the Creek") along Hangman Creek twenty-five miles to the northeast of Steptoe Butte. Another is that Cashup may have turned to the first sawmill constructed on the Palouse. William Codd and carpenter M. J. Sexton had taken a rudimentary single-blade sawmill in Colfax and transformed it into a more efficient sawmill kept busy by the growing demands of Palouse pioneers. However, Cashup's hotel lumber came from a different source. A man named Luther Kerns had the skills Cashup needed and a remarkable plan. More on that shortly.

It was not just the beams, struts, and siding he needed. Cashup's hotel needed to be as lavish as possible. There were nice hotels already functioning in Colfax, Walla Walla, and Spokane Falls, but Cashup wanted his to be the best of them all. He contracted with Roberts & Ford to supply his millwork from their specialized sawmill in Colfax. Style and grace would define the hotel inside and out.

Third step, lumber, accomplished.

Road

No one had ever built a road up Steptoe Butte. It was unclear whether doing so was even possible with construction equipment of the day. There were no motor-driven vehicles back then: just horses to pull the blades to carve out the steep hill-side, which, incidentally, was solid rock for a great portion of the route. Erickson wrote that the road building "was a horse and scraper, pick and shovel job and a major engineering accomplishment. James (Cashup) Davis designed the entire project himself." Would the hill prove too steep for the horses to haul wagons loaded with supplies and (later) guests all the way up? To eliminate as much of that as possible, a *Colfax Gazette* reminiscence on March 17, 1911, stated that for $1,200 Cashup constructed a road with sharp switchbacks "winding up the south side" of Steptoe Butte. Other accounts said he spent far more on the impossible road. So harrowing was the journey that some people closed their eyes to avoid looking down the steep grade, which lay just inches away. Cashup planned for guests to take their own horses and wagons up the butte or, because space at the summit was limited, to hop on Cashup's hired wagons—not unlike a shuttle today.

Fourth step, the road to the summit, accomplished.

Construction

One of the best decisions Cashup made was to hire Luther Kerns to lead construction. While some historical accounts and relics often claim that "Cashup built the hotel," it is more accurate to say that Cashup conceived of the hotel and Kerns and his crew built it. Kerns's team included Joe Seahorn, S. P. Kieler, and a man named Stark.

Kerns, an accomplished builder, had already built a few structures on the Palouse, including one of its earliest schoolhouses. He constructed the Matlock bridge over the Palouse River by "hewing the 60-foot girders for the bridge with a broadax from timber grown where Elberton [Idaho] now stands," per Kerns's daughter, Ida Kerns Dennis, who later wrote a proud and charming piece about her father. "Spokane contractors said it would be impossible to build a structure which would withstand the winds at that point,"

Nick Manring, from a famed pioneer family, holds two handmade nails used in the construction of Cashup's hotel. These have been passed down within his family. Photograph by Jeff Burnside

wrote Ida. Since her father was experienced at planing his own timber, which he had done for his own family home and likely for other projects, he did not have to contract with a sawmill. "Every bit of timber and lumber was hauled from Elberton to the foot of the butte," his daughter noted. That was in 1887. The author of an 1892 article in the Albany, Oregon, *Democrat* describes a sawmill in Elberton with a "20,000 [board] feet capacity per day," but it is not clear whether the sawmill began operation at the time Kerns was building Davis's hotel. It is possible that, rather incredibly, Kerns planed Cashup's timber near where they cut it down in

Elberton before his team hauled it all to the base of Steptoe Butte. This method meant that running raw timber down the Palouse River to the Colfax sawmill, as was the practice, was unnecessary.

Planing your own lumber for such a massive construction project was an audacious undertaking. But Kerns was that good, that industrious. He had homesteaded just ten years before in Tennessee Flats, a popular area of the Palouse very near Steptoe Butte and nine miles north of Colfax, where many pioneers arriving from Tennessee, fueled by word of mouth, tended to settle. Luther's wife died while his children were quite young, but he cared for them fastidiously with the help of relatives until he remarried three years later to a woman who became just like a mother to his children. Prior to that he fought for the Union side in the Civil War, serving with his father in a regiment from Iowa. Kerns was well traveled and came to the Palouse by way of Indiana; Iowa; Illinois; San Jose, California; and Salem, Oregon, to settle at last in Tennessee Flats. Ida writes that her father had gone ahead of the family to find land on the Palouse. When they arrived three months later, on November 4, 1878, by covered wagon, "we saw the homestead for the first time. My father had erected a box house, 14 by 16 feet, and battened on the outside to cover the cracks. He had ceiled [sic] the interior of the house with tongued and grooved lumber, which he planed and prepared himself. In the cabin there was a new stove, bought from Livingston & Kuhn, Colfax; two home-made bedsteads and four benches, artistically made. Chairs were too expensive to be thought of at this time. After buying a five-gallon can of kerosene oil we had just 75 cents left with which to begin the winter. By the way, this can of oil represented $7. We, therefore, found it expedient to retire early to save oil."

Kerns immediately began making a name for himself, writes his daughter. "Mother and I were left to hold down the ranch while father went back to Colfax to work for Lippitt Brothers and also put in shelving for the Livingston & Kuhn Hardware store. In this way, he was able to provide food for us during the winter and also save some money with which to purchase farming implements for use when spring arrived." Because educating his children was important, he built the schoolhouse in Tennessee Flats and helped hire its first teacher through twenty-five-cent membership fees.

Kerns's relatives lived on the Palouse and all were deeply involved in religious activities. He visited every neighbor within a ten-mile radius to invite them to his home for Sunday School classes, too, Ida wrote. So many attended—as many as forty-five—that he had to move things out of his home to accommodate the crowd. He also hosted itinerant preachers going through the region. One of those traveling pastors was Milton Wright, a bishop with the Church of the United Brethren in Christ, who wrote fastidiously in his daily notebook:

"Saturday, June 11[.] Bro. Evans goes to Colfax, and I go to Elberton afoot, about 3 ½ ms. Dinner and lodging at Luther Kerns', a brother of Rev. H. O. Kerns. He['s] a[n] M. E. [Methodist Episcopalian][.] His wife a U. B. [United Brethren.] In afternoon, study some on a sermon on Rom. 8:21. Stay at Kern's," which he did for several nights.

After returning back East to his large family at home, Bishop Wright and his wife finished raising five children, including two little boys, nicknamed "The Bishop's Kids," Orville and Wilbur Wright. The man who built Cashup's hotel had hosted the man who gave birth to the inventors of the airplane.

Now Kerns was dealing with a nonfamilial famous acquaintance—Cashup Davis. And word was getting out about the lavish hotel.

"'Cash-up' Davis will put men to work on his Aerial hotel on the summit of Steptoe Butte, as soon as the weather will admit," declared a Spokane Falls newspaper on February 9, 1888. "This enterprising gentleman is determined to make this a first-class resort for sight-seers, and invalids who need pure and bracing air."

"All the timber and rafters were securely bolted together" for the demanding slow haul "up the steep mountain," Ida wrote. Kerns and Cashup reduced the wind force on the building, which sat vulnerably on the hill's pinnacle, by adding "a deck roof to ease the force of the wind over the building." It was a wise design solution that also allowed for a grand observatory on the third floor.

"Contracts have been let for the erection of several buildings on Steptoe Butte by Mr. Davis and [it] is expected they will be ready for the tourist travel of the coming summer. The main building will be 60 x 64 feet [some references vary in size depending on whether a porch was included] and will cost $5,000. It will be finished with a view to beauty and comfort and will doubtless be a popular resort for pleasure parties and tourists," said the *Colfax Gazette* on May 2, 1888. "Mr. Davis has already graded an excellent road to the summit of the butte and erected buildings for the workmen to live in, and carpenters and graders are busy at work. He expects to have everything ready by the Fourth of July."

Scheduling the hotel's grand opening for the Fourth of July was a wise marketing move. It was both in celebration of the country that had given him so much and extra excuse to double down on the festive holiday atmosphere. But, like so much of what Cashup set his mind to, it required astounding logistical problem solving, especially after a disaster struck the construction site. "An army of carpenters was constructing a spacious building on the summit . . . while the people looked on in amazement."

It happened the last week of April 1888, as reported in the *Washington Standard* on June 1: "One day last week while workmen on 'Cashup' Davis' new building on Steptoe Butte were engaged in raising several heavy truss timbers to the second story the great weight caused a portion of the frame to give way and three men were precipitated violently to the ground, together with the frame work of the building. As soon as possible the men were extricated from the debris and removed to places of comfort while a messenger was dispatched to Colfax for surgical assistance. Luther Kerns, the contractor, was cut severely on the forehead, and bruised on one hip. Joseph Seahorn suffered a fracture of the little finger on the left hand, and his right leg was severely bruised. S. P. Kieler's injuries were the most serious. He was senseless when taken from the ruins, and suffered from a deep scalp wound on the back of his head. His body was badly bruised also, and internal injuries [are] feared. All the men were greatly shocked by the fall, besides their other injuries."

After such a massive setback, the question had to be asked: Would they finish by the Fourth of July? Or worse: Could this project ever be built in such a challenging location?

Despite this cloud of uncertainty, all the region's newspapers—as far away as Seattle 300 miles to the west—kept raising excitement, and expectations. "A grand celebration will be held on Steptoe Butte July 4th, under the auspices of 'Cashup' Davis." . . . "Within a very short time Steptoe will present an inviting place for pleasure seekers."

Still, Cashup needed to think of that essential piece to bring people in. He knew how to get people talking and soon identified a hotel feature that would not only inspire newspaper coverage but also draw visitors—the panoramic view of the Palouse that only the hotel offered. Indeed, in addition to its dazzling rooms, dances, and dinner events, this was a hotel with a very special view.

The view. That's it. Cashup would capitalize even more on the extraordinary view from atop Steptoe Butte by buying the most powerful telescope he could find and affix it in the hotel observatory. Wanting only the best, Cashup bought what was called "the second most powerful telescope" in the territory. (Curiously, we don't know which telescope might have been the most powerful or perhaps it was Cashup's advertising bluster.) Made of brass and mounted onto a strong wooden tripod, Cashup's telescope measured about four feet long, perhaps five inches in diameter. It was an objective-style telescope: to see the view, one looked in through the eyepiece and out the large lens at the end. Attached to the side near the eyepiece was the finder.

Cashup's telescope had been made in Paris by the optical firm Bardou and Son. This type of telescope was first seen in the eastern United States in 1880, so Cashup had acquired one of the most modern and advanced telescopes available. It had an 800-millimeter lens called an "objective F-10" with a simple refractor. Cashup wanted his guests to see the distance and the vista through this telescope on the Steptoe Butte vantage point.

Once again, Cashup spared no expense. Written accounts lavished praise on it. Roberts wrote that the magnificent telescope cost Cashup $300, while the *Colfax Gazette* reported it cost $450. Either way, Cashup was on a spending spree, driven by an obsession for "the big idea," as newspaperman Allen called it. Acquiring this magnificent telescope and mounting it at the top of the hotel on the summit of the highest peak around would, on a clear day, enabled his guests to see Walla Walla and Spokane and at least three mountain ranges as well as all the homes and farms within a hundred miles.

It was still not clear, however, that Cashup could open on July 4. And how would his fellow pioneers respond to the new hotel? He was about to find out whether the marketplace, rivalries, and even jealousy-turned-gossip would prevent the realization of his dream.

The unavoidable fact remained: Cashup was now seventy-two years old. He had the vision. He had the ambition. He had the money. But did he have the stamina? Could he maintain his health and his energy to finish? Could he survive this ordeal?

The only known photograph of Mary Ann and Cashup together on the steep and rocky slope of Steptoe Butte. She did not like the summit and rarely visited. From the Davis Family.

Cashup's hotel as it would have looked when completed. Illustration by Noah Kroese.

NINE

THE GRAND OPENING

The mountain became a motto to the man.

New York Evening Post

CASHUP DAVIS STOOD ON THE 14-by-14-foot cupola atop his new hotel. Perched on the highest point in all the Palouse—a butte he now owned—he looked out over every homestead and every town from horizon to horizon. "A land of peace and plenty." His lavish hotel was ready to open with great fanfare on July 4, 1888, honoring the birthday of his adopted nation.

At that very moment, he had a lifetime on which to reflect. The confident, short, British kid who came to the United States with an obsession for the American West was now standing over a region which was the very definition of the western edge of settlement. He had beaten the odds. He had proven his doubters wrong. He had stuck to his vision. His heart was full. Cashup could be forgiven for feeling like a king.

Indeed, the castles that surrounded him during his childhood in southern England did plausibly inspire him to build one of his own, albeit as a hotel. Indeed, the hotel was his castle, high on a butte.

Residents all around the Palouse and newspapers throughout the region anticipated the dazzling structure's opening day. "A balloon ascension and fireworks will be features of the occasion, while the evening will be devoted to dancing," reported the *Lewiston Teller* and *Seattle Post-Intelligencer*. "Within a short time

Steptoe will be the most attractive place for a visitor in the whole inland country," reported the *Spokane Review.*

A handful of references exist regarding the cost of the hotel, its land, the road, its interiors, and its furnishings. Expenses ranged from $5,000 for the road alone to $20,000 for the entire project. Needless to say, in 1888 that was a lot of money. And Cashup, so determined, spent it. Pioneers must have looked on in envy that someone could complete such a project. As one newspaper put it, "he was known as the money king of the Palouse country."

When guests arrived, the first sight they encountered upon entering the front doors was a large, ornate ballroom that dominated the main floor at 60 feet long and 44 feet wide, a space that also included a kitchen and stage.

The chamber size easily could accommodate performances of all kinds to dazzle guests, and soon the hotel calendar filled with various groups and events to host, including orchestras, vocal performers, musical recitals, Chautauqua features, Punch and Judy shows of the era, and of course the "magic lantern" show whose viewfinder used smoke, mirrors, and focused sources of light (two years before electricity came to nearby Farmington) to enhance lodgers' visual pleasure. Two dressing rooms on either side of the stage gave it all a professional air.

If he hadn't qualified as such before, Cashup now had become, with his stylish hotel, a one-man chamber of commerce. Any inch of space afforded an opportunity to promote something about the community. Indeed, an alcove near the entrance displayed the various crops of the Palouse, "beautifully decorated with all the grains, fruits and cereals that are available in this country." The bounty was meticulously bundled and hung from metal bars attached to the high ceiling, with tables and shelves stocked with large vases and tin cans of all sizes containing more crops. On the walls, framed sketches of world-famous people, bridges, boulevards, steamships, and cities (including a scene of

The hotel's ballroom, 1888. Note the wheat and other crops suspended from the ceiling as well as displays on the low wall dividers. From the collection of Jim Martin.

New York Harbor near Pier 15 where Cashup had arrived from England) added a wider awareness, a sense of how the world's industrial grandeur and possibility connected to Steptoe—that the Palouse was right up there with the big boys. It was all so "Cashup."

Guests ringed the ballroom from a balcony above, looking down at the dancing and hubbub below. The second floor also had a dining room for fifty people. From that balcony, guests accessed their rooms, "fitted up in comfortable style and every convenience and attraction . . . to make time pass in this great northwestern pleasure resort like a happy dream." As they walked through the rest of the hotel, they saw hand-carved wood trim—an elegance that made them feel like they were in the finest quarters of Paris or New York. No, the hotel was not by any means as ornate as the world's great hotels. But its appearance made these tough pioneers feel pretty special.

The most important guests were invited into a lounge that served as Cashup's private quarters—a VIP room of sorts, reserved for more intimate conversations. Its contents showcased moments in Cashup's life. A photograph shows him sporting his trimmed white beard, sitting upright in an ornate armchair wearing a full suit, vest, white shirt, and tie. His fingers hold his place in an open book that rests on his knee. On the walls are personally important items:

- An illustration of a three-masted schooner plying a turbulent sea. Cashup came to America aboard the vessel *Quebec*, similar to the one displayed in the image.
- A photograph in which a lone soldier stands, clad in a ceremonial uniform complete with sash, medals, and bearskin hat—one of those tall, furry black hats British guards still wear. The photograph includes no visible description, so it is impossible to say whether the figure is his uncle, Col. William Short, who introduced him to the military elite and aristocracy, or Capt. John Gwynn, with whom Cashup toured much of England and beyond in his early years. But Cashup's attachment to it is likely because it is clearly reminiscent of his life in Britain.
- A state-of-the-art heating stove. Elaborate stoves like this were quite new and all the rage, but rare in the settled West in 1888. Cashup bought the latest model made by the Peninsular Stove Company, with metal moldings of Western history's great men adorning its front edges. He likely ordered it from one of the stores in Colfax and had it shipped in at great expense aboard one of the new railroad lines that allowed for

transportation of very heavy items. Peninsular was one of the biggest and most prestigious manufacturers of metal stoves in America. The company was based in Detroit, capital of a burgeoning stove industry that, in a few years, pivoted to making automobiles, one of America's greatest industries.

- A microscope, placed on the main table. As was the convention in the late 1800s, the microscopes angled straight down for viewing specimens. Cashup's was a fine one, with a rotating specimen tray and angled reflective light source to illuminate the bottom of the specimen. Like many pioneers, Cashup took reading and learning seriously.

- A stereoscope (photo viewer). Placed next to Cashup's microscope, the device presented double images to users, giving the impression of a three-dimensional image.

- His beloved sword. The weapon had been given to him as a boy by his uncle Col. William Short. Cashup took it with him when he crossed the Atlantic and subsequently to the American West. In the photograph, it appears mounted on the wall over his right shoulder. I will never forget the first time I held Cashup's sword. I felt as close to him as I would ever get, knowing how much the weapon meant to him.

- Cashup's top hat and cane, carefully placed a few feet away from his chair. Men of style wore top hats and used canes back then, even though it may have seemed a bit out of place in the rough-and-tumble Palouse. Nearly all the outdoor photos of Cashup show him wearing his top hat. The hat shown in this photo, identifiable by its very specific blemishes, is also on display in Colfax. It had passed from Cashup to his son Charley ("C. J."), to my dad Aubrey, to my brother

Cashup in his private quarters in the hotel, 1888. From the collection of Jim Martin.

Dave, and then to me. Even though Cashup had a small head and I am a pretty stocky fellow, I tried it on. I felt proud, like I was wearing a piece of history. It was an uplifting experience. No, it didn't fit. Not even close. Cashup was not a big guy. But he had presence.

• A dog. Perhaps the most unusual item shown in the famous photo of Cashup in his private parlor is a dog. Yes, Cashup had a small dog, a rather strange-looking one, sitting dutifully by his feet posing and looking straight into the camera. The presence of a pet dog, especially in those days, is rare and says a lot about Cashup. He was known for his kindness to people and to animals—even his chickens, geese, and other livestock, which he named and let wander in and out of the family home and outbuildings.

> A grand celebration will be held on
> Steptoe Butte July 4th, under the aus-
> pices of "Cashup" Davis. A balloon as
> cension and fireworks will be features of
> the occasion, while the evening will be
> devoted to dancing. The new hotel on the
> butte will be opened that day and the
> public is cordially invited. A peep
> through the big telescope is worth the
> 25 cents charge for admission.—*Gazette.*

Announcement of the hotel's opening in the *Lewiston Teller* newspaper, 1888. From Newspapers.com.

Unsurprisingly, Cashup worked the crowd during the grand opening, "beguiling his visitors" and making them feel welcome, as he had done so successfully while running his stage stop. The hotel was crowded with more than a hundred people, based on photographs of the event. "In all that time of stress," wrote Roberts, "he met every guest as though he were a notable dignitary and entertained him royally."

Cashup must have known he was making history and he pulled out all the stops. Of course, he also knew about word-of-mouth advertising—especially on this crucial day. It was his forte. Great customer experiences beget more customers, especially when lavished with amenities of refined living. Once again, he demonstrated the pursuit of excellence. Cashup hired a ten-piece horn section and a percussionist, likely led by Cy and Andy Privett of Colfax, who had been so popular at his stage stop. The guests celebrated under the fireworks and the hot-air balloon ascension and kept dancing until dawn.

His first day was a smashing success. And it portended a future of near-certain popularity. Cashup wisely followed up on it by commissioning an 1888 version of a shuttle van to provide

Grand opening of the hotel on July 4, 1888. Note that the railing on the roof terrace is not yet completed. From the Whitman County Historical Society, Perkins House, Colfax, WA.

transport for guests up that sometimes harrowing, winding road to the summit. Carved into steep slopes, the dusty path wrapped around the butte several times, switching back and forth, on its upward snake, tempting those daring enough with a heart-stopping view just outside the stagecoach window. It would be bad for business if people worried too much about the precarious road to the top. So Cashup also hired the best and most widely known stagecoach driver on the Palouse to run his guests from the old stage stop a few miles from the butte to the summit, where they were dropped off right at the front door like royalty. As only he could do, Cashup, a celebrity in his own right, hired a celebrity stage driver to run the shuttle. His name was Miles Kelly Hill. Everyone knew him by his nickname, Shorty. He had driven stage for the legendary Felix Warren, which frequently traveled to Cashup's stage stop. Shorty had a reputation for being the best bronco rider and stagecoach driver around. And he was, like Cashup, entertaining, on the short side, and full of charisma.

"It's pretty darn steep at the top and pretty narrow," says Dave Wahl, eighty, a cowboy poet from Genesee, Idaho, who, as a young boy, grew up listening to Shorty's extraordinary stories. Shorty's tales included Cashup's hotel. "In those days, it was all gravel, and it was more narrow and steeper and more wind-y," says Wahl. He describes Shorty thus: "He was bowlegged as a wish bone, you could walk a pony through."

Shorty not only drove stage all over the Inland Empire but he also starred in bucking bronco shows. One of Wahl's poems suggests Cashup hired the right guy to calm any anxiety. "He drove stage to Cashup Davis's grand hotel on Steptoe Butte. He could ride while bucking horses. And he knew how to shoot. He'd ride those bucking horses and gesture toward the stands, while rolling pointy-ended cigarettes with his free left hand."

Business at the hotel continued at a robust clip day after day, although historical writings suggest it closed for the winters when snow and ice and bitter winds at the summit—and the roads to it—made it unpleasant at best.

Photography was still uncommon in the 1880s, but one day early on Cashup gathered 114 guests, family members, and friends to pose for a photo outside the hotel. There are conflicting dates attributed to the photo. Scribbled in white on the photograph, as was normal back then, a hand-drawn scroll announces, "Steptoe Butte 3800 feet high. The best place in Washington to get a good view of the country." Then to the right, the same scribbler wrote, "we are waiting for the car." To the far left, a surrey without a horse waits. Perhaps it was Shorty's, waiting to take guests back down the butte that day.

In the foreground, a ladder and stone rubble suggest the photo may indeed have been taken on the day of the grand opening. People stand shoulder to shoulder in front of the hotel, with still more lining the cupola on the third floor. A ten-piece horn band with a drummer performs to guests in their finest: men in dark suits, white shirts, and dark bowler hats, women in long full dresses tightly fitted around the torso, their heads festooned with big flapping hats.

Sitting in front is Cashup, visible in the sea of dark suits by his cloud-white hair and beard. A woman leans toward him in fawning fashion. It likely isn't Mary Ann because she did not spend much time up there. Newspapers and other records identify the women sitting next to Cashup in the photo as Lula Mae Jennings McMeekin (who married one of Cashup's grandchildren a few years later), Margaret K. Inman Jennings, and Ada Mae Jennings Davis.

"I remember Barney O'Neil . . . Charles Hinchclif . . . and I attended the dance after Cash-Up Davis finished his hotel and dance hall," wrote O. N. Bell in his pioneer remembrance. "Mr. Davis also told us where Col. Steptoe fought the Indians on the top of Steptoe butte some years before." As noted previously, this story is not true, but Cashup would not let the truth get in the way of a good story.

The main attraction of the hotel was Cashup. But the second bill perched at the top, inside the observatory and reading room: the large brass telescope. In 1888, people had never seen anything like it. The *Lewiston Teller* and *Seattle Post-Intelligencer* pronounced: "A peep through the big telescope is worth the 25 cents charge for admission."

Just after the grand opening, an authoritative book described the telescope's amazing powers. "With its aid, a view, scarcely to be paralleled in the country . . . spread[s] out like a map. A foreground of vast rolling plains checkered with grain fields; a background of towering mountains, rising, tier on tier, till they break at last against the barriers of eternal frost—such is the outlook which daily greets the vision of this brave old pioneer of the Palouse." Some called the device "Cash-up's Pride."

"I have visited the summit of Steptoe many times," wrote Roberts. "My first visit was made soon after completion of the building. Early one morning, late in June, we drove a tallyho [a fast horse-drawn coach] up the mountain, stabled and fed our four horses and climbed the stairway to the observatory. The wind was whist [silent], visibility superb. The first impression, which, I have learned, is common under similar conditions, is most striking. Though the elevation is over 3600 feet, at least 1000 feet above the surround base, one does not sense the elevation for there are no comparable heights nearby. One seems to be at the bottom of a vast saucer-like depression, bordered by an undulated horizon line, encircling a region extending roughly a radial distance of a hundred miles. The whole vast scope in a continuous patchwork of browning pasture, black fallow ground, green fields of spring-sown grain, ripening fields of winter wheat and all dotted with plantings of orchard and shade trees, with streams meandering at will over all."

S. C. Roberts wrote it this way: "Invoking the aid of the $300 telescope with its six inch objective lens, you may bring to view the dome of the convent at Pendleton, Oregon, on the south, a hundred miles away; the spires of Ritzville, 60 miles, and the ridge of the Big Bend plateau 30 miles farther to the west; the summits of the Coeur d'Alene mountains 40 miles east and the smokestacks of the Hillyard car shops 50 miles to the north. It is easy to look down into 30 towns, in some of which you may read the store signs."

Many decades later, pioneers of the time still remembered Cashup's hotel fondly. In 1972, David G. Kuehl wrote, "I first visited the hotel back in 1899 or 1900 and have revisited this spot many times since. It seems to hold a special attachment to me."

Even family historian Julia Davis Eckhart, who was born after the hotel was built and grew up hearing the stories, wrote years later, "I heard there were some wild times up there."

Hotel ballroom circa 1890, with Reverend Todd and Reverend Sproat sitting among the agricultural displays. From the collection of Jim Martin.

"When Mr. Davis purchased this historical hill many of his friends thought he was out of his head, but those who have visited the place have changed their minds wonderfully," gushed the *Spokane Review*. "Cash Up can not be other than voted an enterprising and progressive man. His advertising the butte as he is not only benefits himself, but the entire country and community."

Cashup knew he had a good thing going. And he sought to invest in his hotel and his Steptoe Butte operations with more improvements and events. Around 1890, he added a covered porch around the entire hotel that was ten feet deep, creating more floor space for large crowds and allowing people to relax outside while taking in the stunning view.

During the hotel's construction, Cashup and his team dug a cistern to hold water for hotel operations. But it wasn't big enough. It also was likely located under the hotel itself, so expanding it was not an option. As a result, his staff had to haul water regularly up the steep grade—not a good situation.

Cashup planned a convention at the hotel to bring together Indian leaders and American historians to clarify that, contrary to popular belief at the time, the Battle of Pine Creek had not taken place on Steptoe Butte. He knew he could not claim that his hotel was the site of this battle, but it could surely be the site of that discussion! Brilliant.

In May 1891, Cashup hosted a "temperance ball" at the hotel, celebrating the era's push against alcohol. The period was called "the second wave of temperance." Alcohol was a problem in many areas of the United States, including the pioneer West where saloons were plentiful. Fundamentalist religion was quite prevalent on the Palouse and local churches worked toward temperance. Farmhands too often got drunk the night before a big harvest. And domestic violence was a serious problem because men who lorded over their household and were drunk to boot might physically harm their wives and children. Cashup's hotel, and his stage stop before that, was known for parties and good times, so Cashup was eager to demonstrate to the community that they could have fun without alcohol. Drunkenness, however, would cause an embarrassing story for Cashup, which we will cover later in this book.

Cashup organized at least one event to bring children to the hotel ballroom, giving it a family feeling and likely appealing to all those parents.

He also announced additional work on the grounds at the summit; twin terraces ninety square feet each with grand stairs that descended one to the other, fully landscaped, although this work was never done.

Cashup's apple trees, planted along the slopes of the butte, were mature and in full production now. As a result of his wise varietal planting, he provided his hotel guests with fresh apples many months during harvest season.

The success of the hotel paralleled the expansion and productivity of the Palouse. Electricity lines were gradually built.
Cars were still more than a decade away, but new railroad
lines continued to slice the region, boosting commerce and
bringing more people to the area. The Washington Territory
became the State of Washington just seventeen months after
the hotel opened.

One newspaper account said Cashup was considering building a monument to pioneers at the top of the butte. And he told
many people that he wanted to be buried at the summit, even
having a shovel with which he himself would someday dig his
own grave.

Cashup had achieved such prominence that there "has been considerable discussion [i]n the various local papers concerning the name
of a noted landmark" about renaming Steptoe Butte as "Cashup's
Butte," or some such name. There is no record of Cashup himself
promoting this idea—at least not publicly, although one account
does allege it was his idea. Indeed, the discussion began even while
the hotel was under construction. The nearby newspaper, *Garfield
Enterprise*, chimed in early on, endorsing the name change.

But, as almost anyone who achieves great success can attest,
Cashup had detractors. And it got a little ugly. The ugliest may
have come from the *Spangle Record*, which wrote a scathing, personal attack on Cashup, saying "Mr. Davis was high cockalorem
in the Palouse country," an old phrase which means a little man
who incorrectly has a very high opinion of himself; someone
low-level and unimportant.

Ouch. It got worse. The writer accused Cashup of taking
advantage of farmers desperate for cash, claiming he famously
offered to pay in cash but would then use the cash offer to get a
low price, haggle the price further downward, and then make the
deal—but only paying half in cash and half "in a few days when
the Portland mail comes." Without attribution, the article said,

"One settler says men have grown old and died of old age waiting for the 'balance' on the 'Cash-Up' trade."

Jacob and Frederick Schorr, publishers of the *Northwest Tribune* based in Cheney and later Spokane, wrote another nasty article. They claimed Jacob had been in a group traveling from Colfax to Cheney on a hot day. "They stopped at the notorious Cash-up Davis [stage stop] to get a drink of water for themselves and horses. Cash-Up immediately made his appearance and ordered them away and without allowing them to use the water running from his spring." It ended: "The sooner he is forgotten the better."

Experts on success and enterprise say achievement comes with detractors. They urge successful people to see the haters as a sign of that success. Energy comes from knowing that detractors are responding to their own failures. They are envious of your sunshine and tired of their own shade. Given Cashup's abundant self-confidence—not arrogance—he likely drew energy from his detractors and pushed even harder.

"The energy and interest he displayed in his new undertaking was wonderful to behold," said Virgil McCroskey, the successful son of Cashup's neighbor and fellow pioneer J. P. T. McCroskey. "He wanted a site where people could come from near or far away and view the scenic beauties of the land he loved so well."

"In his determination to make a success of his Steptoe resort, Cashup Davis devoted the energies of his declining years; not, as I see it, so much for prospective gain, as for the sheer joy of achieving the development of a delightful lookout and playhouse," wrote Roberts.

A New York newspaper reporter put it this way:

I think in some way "Cashup" and Steptoe drew little by little nearer together, because they are so similar. Both are sturdy, upright, downright individuals, maintaining the dignity of higher plateaus amid the lower range by

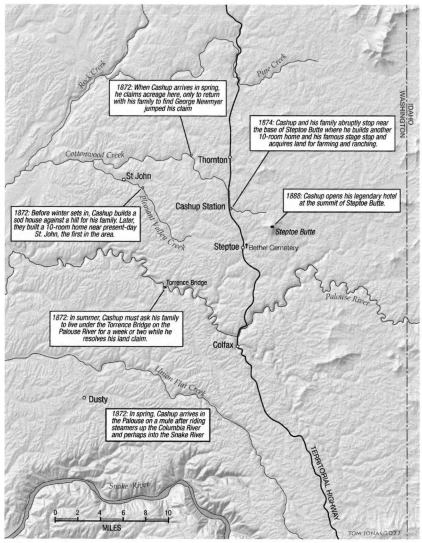

Key locations on the Palouse in the life of James "Cashup" Davis. Map by Tom Jonas.

which they are surrounded. The subtle air or the swift wind could not affect the integrity of either. I think somehow the mountain became a motto to the man, and he demanded from and gave to his neighbors its sheer and undeviating honesty.

The *Spokane Falls Review* wrote of Cashup and his successful hotel, "there he has built an imperishable monument to himself in the form of his observatory and other buildings [overlooking] the fertile land at the foot of his castle."

What made the hotel so special was that it perched on top of one of the greatest heights on the Palouse. Yet, that great height would also be its greatest downfall, as Cashup was about to learn.

TEN

WHEN MARY ANN DIED

A man can overcome any obstacle and accomplish any goal if he believes his wife believes in him.

DAVE WILLIS, MARRIAGE EXPERT

THERE IS NO OTHER WAY to put it: according to multiple accounts, Mary Ann Davis simply did not like spending her time at the hotel in its remote location on top of the butte. She was now approaching her late sixties and, by the 1890s, she was a grandmother many times over. (Her eldest grandchild was in his twenties.) Leaving the hotel to go anywhere on the Palouse required an arduous horse and buggy descent of the butte, followed invariably by an arduous ascent back up upon return.

The Davises still owned their home, farm, and outbuildings at the old stage stop several miles from the base of the butte, where there was always work to be done. Mary Ann was immensely proud of her vegetable garden and orchard—"the most beautiful" on the Palouse, she said, and others agreed. She wanted to spend more time with her grown children and their families who lived all over the Palouse, including Oakesdale, the town nearest the butte.

Mary Ann and Cashup had been married for nearly fifty years. As one might expect, she had a few health issues, so being off

One of the only known photographs of Mary Ann Davis,
Cashup's wife. From the Davis Family.

the butte made it safer and easier to get whatever medical care
she needed. You may recall Mary Ann's letter, written during the
so-called Indian Scare of 1877, which included her statement:
"My health is poor, my heart troubles me. I sure hope I get better
soon." It was perhaps part medical fact, part expression of loneli-
ness. But ten years later, her ill health had continued.

Cashup held the spotlight in their marriage. She never made
headlines like her gregarious husband did, nor did she want to.
But her family and descendants held deep respect for her. She was

Cashup's rock; who knows how many of his ideas she nixed before they ever saw the light of day? "She was the unsung hero," says Mary Ann's great-great-granddaughter Pat Mick. Amy Charlotte Davis, Mary Ann's youngest child and great-grandmother to Pat, lived until 1961 and shared endless stories and insights about her parents. So infused with admiration was Mick that she wrote a posthumous letter to Mary Ann. It was a way of showing her admiration for the woman she had heard so much about, who was so important to their family, but whom Mick had never met.

"Mary Ann, you must have been quite a mother and wife," began the letter. "This contemporary descendant cannot imagine raising eleven children without modern day conveniences." Women, especially, seem to be astonished with Mary Ann, who had to follow her husband and move her family seven times from Ohio across the Midwest to the Far West and Palouse. Moving from the base of Steptoe Butte up to the "castle" at the top may have been the shortest of all the moves they made, but it was also the most audacious.

In early summer 1894, Mary Ann grew "dangerously sick" and moved in with thirty-two-year-old daughter Mary Ann Davis Martin and her husband George Martin in Oakesdale, on the edge of town near where they had a farm. Over the course of several months, her downward slide continued. Doctors cared for her; friends visited her and prayed for her. Reverend Edward H. Todd of the M. E. Church in Colfax, a family friend, came to give her comfort. She had never been a religious woman but now "she professed her trust in Christ."

On about October 1, 1894, Mary Ann Davis passed away. Her husband Cashup, her large family, and many friends and neighbors were there during her final days.

"Death of Mrs. Davis: A Long Life of Good Work Ended Last Week," announced the *Garfield Enterprise* a few days later. "She was a mother to her children, always looking after their comfort and happiness. She took pleasure in making home happy. She was pronounced by her neighbors and those who knew her best a good neighbor. Always kind to the sick and ready to administer to their comfort. She delighted in accommodating those around her." The perfect partner for a man like Cashup.

So beloved was Mary Ann that "the church was well filled with friends and neighbors." "Whatever your hand finds to do, do it with all your might," recited Reverend Todd to the assembled. The passage he read from, Ecclesiastes 9:10, reminds us to labor hard during our one life on earth, a fitting way to honor Mary Ann for her life of noble honest work.

Three months after her death, a loving voice that had been absent for many years from the Davis household arrived. Sivyer Davis, Cashup's younger brother, with whom he had sailed to America all those years ago, mailed a touching letter from his home in Hillsboro, Kansas, to one of Mary Ann's sons. (The letter, dated January 1, 1895, opens only with "Dear Nephew," but the rest of the text gives clues that the addressee was either John Franklin Davis or William Davis.) Sivyer said of her death: "That is the worst thing that ever happened in that family. You must all of you miss her very much. That smiling and welcome face to you all. When you went over their [sic] you see no more. If I should come over their [sic] I should miss her almost as much as you do for I knew her so well[.] [In] her younger days [we] lived near together for years we always agreed very well never had any trouble and I always felt at home when I was at her house. How does my Brother get along now." Even though Sivyer admitted in the letter that he and Cashup rarely communicated, he knew how much Mary Ann meant to the family and to Cashup.

She was buried in Bethel Cemetery, a beautiful hill with a sweeping view of Steptoe Butte, a peaceful place where many settlers of the period are buried.

The home of Mary Ann (Davis) Martin in Oakesdale, WA, 1890. This is the house where her mother Mary Ann (Shoemaker) Davis died in October 1894, after a long illness. In 2021, we visited this house and walked the creaky staircases imagining the family gathered for her final days. From the collection of Jim Martin, restored.

Leoti L. West, the well-known writer and reporter of Palouse pioneer stories, wrote in the early 1900s that "Mrs. Davis was a plain, wholesome, competent woman who made a most charming hostess."

"Many tribute words have been written about your husband. But I really applaud you Mary Ann," wrote Mick in her letter 130 years later. "Underneath Cashup's gregarious personality which gained him fame, was a woman who quietly led 'the steadfast charge' of maintaining a family. Your children must have seen all this for themselves as well. I do." With regard to Mary Ann's demand that the family halt the trip to Canada, Mick wrote "I would have said more than, 'stop the wagons,' great-great-grand-mother. You must have been one 'helluva' woman, my dear."

All of Mary Ann's eleven adult children mourned her death. She was the first of their clan to die. As happens in every family, the seemingly inviolable unit experienced its first loss. But at least now her legacy could shine.

You may recall earlier mention that Mary Ann's family, the Shoemakers, came from England to Pennsylvania in 1686, nearly a century before the Revolutionary War and 155 years before Cashup landed at Pier 15 in New York. According to Shoemaker family historian and genealogist Benjamin H. Shoemaker III, Mary Ann's ancestors fell on both sides of the angst between the colonies and the British, serving on councils and assemblies supporting differing views. "All the Shoemakers were Quakers," wrote Shoemaker in a touching 1963 letter to Julia Davis Eckhart, granddaughter of Cashup and Mary Ann, "and didn't fight and mostly favor the British because they thought the Colonies started the war. My own ancestor, Robert, did not take the oath of allegiance to the Colonial side until the war was over in 1786—so I assume he was a Tory (he died in the yellow fever epidemic here in 1796)."

On November 14, 2019, 125 years and a few days after my great-grandmother Mary Ann passed away in that white wood-framed farmhouse in Oakesdale, I walked into the very same house for the first time. I had a kind of eerie feeling as I entered. I wanted to honor her, to know her, and to stand in the spot where Mary Ann said goodbye to the world. It was where Cashup, all their kids and grandkids, neighbors, and friends had also visited to give their love to this wonderful woman. A welcoming man named Josh Robinson lives with his family in the handsome old home now. They are keenly aware of its history, but I doubt they expected to be asked to give a tour for Mary Ann and Cashup's descendants.

On that beautiful sunshine-drenched, late fall day, my grandson Reese and Jim Martin visited the home with me. Jim is the great-grandson of Mary Davis Martin, who had lived in this house and taken care of her ailing mother until the end. As a member of the Cashup Crew, Jim plays a key role in researching Davis family history and finding and restoring old photos.

Josh welcomed us inside. The house, with only minor changes, appears the reliable, pragmatic farmhouse found on countless other farms in the late 1800s. Once inside, we opened a tiny door, which still retained its original doorknob, to walk up narrow, steep stairs. They creaked with every step. At the top, we turned left to a landing surrounded by four bedrooms. We knew this as the upper floor where Mary Ann's loved ones gathered in quiet somberness to whisper about her fight to live. In one of those tiny bedrooms, Mary Ann, surrounded by her family and perhaps holding the hand of Reverend Todd, took her last breath. There must have been tears, hugs, condolences, and reflections on a worthy life. Eventually, we stepped back down the narrow, creaking staircase and left the house. It was a powerful, poignant moment, and I am grateful to the Robinsons for allowing us to share it.

For the first time since Cashup was a young man, he was without his wife. His children and grandchildren likely turned their attention to helping him maintain his well-being and spirit. He needed it because not only was he dealing with Mary Ann's devastating death, but the hotel was also in trouble.

ELEVEN

DARK HALLWAYS

The only thing harder than becoming the best is staying the best.

ANONYMOUS

THE EVENING OF HIS WIFE'S death, when incessant, chill autumn winds might nudge the temperature below freezing at the top of Steptoe Butte, Cashup opened the door to his hotel and stepped inside. Without his partner for the first time, he stoked the stove and blew out the lamps for his first night truly alone.

The quiet must have been deafening.

During the late fall and winter, the number of visitors and tourists usually waned considerably. So Cashup had been closing the hotel from the first snow until spring. It gave him time for other things: repairs, upgrades, winter farming, visits to nearby cities to promote the hotel. My bet is he read voraciously during these lonely times.

Come better weather, Cashup had always been ready for guests to return, although the truth is as cold as the Palouse snows: with each new spring, fewer and fewer guests would visit the hotel. And those who did arrive in the weeks and months following Mary Ann's death felt obliged to share somber condolences with Cashup. There is often some awkwardness among friends when one of them loses a loved one, especially so because people on vacation come to enjoy themselves, not face the pain of loss.

Things just were not the same. The magic was gone. The novelty of the hotel had long since waned. People were not coming. In addition, America had plunged into the Depression of 1893, whose economic effect impacted the nation for several years. Indeed, it was "a watershed event in American history" fueled, in part, by the boom in agriculture that drove supply up and prices down. Wheat prices tumbled to 20 cents a bushel. Unemployment fell to record levels exceeded only by the Great Depression of the 1930s and the 2020 COVID-19 pandemic. The Rains of '93 on the Palouse only made the situation worse.

With potential customers unemployed or perhaps losing their farms, Cashup's hotel revenue was paltry and did not cover operational costs. The situation was so dire that Cashup even went to the new train station nearby and handed out flyers to passengers, reminding them to come to stay at or at least visit the grand hotel. Alas, it was not enough. In the meantime, Cashup hired a teenager to cut costs and to help with the hotel's upkeep but also, frankly, to keep the widower company. George McCroskey, one of the boys from the renowned pioneer family, who grew up just a road or two over the hill from the Davis family, recounted this heart-wrenching firsthand memory:

"In later years he alone occupied the big house, a lonely and dejected figure, patiently waiting for the crowds which seldom came. When occasional parties ascended the mountain, he would brighten up and was glad, but when they began to leave tears would come to his old eyes. I used to go up often to see and cheer him [up]."

It might be curious to realize that, in the 1890s, people did not call ahead—they couldn't, because there were no telephones. Reservations could be made by mail, but oftentimes guests just showed up. So, the first indication for Cashup that he had guests was when he'd hear horses clip-clopping up the steep road as the wagons neared the summit. He must have done a lot of waiting and wondering. Even then, he still greeted every guest as if he or she were royalty. And he never lost his love of entertaining people. He loved a crowd—even if that crowd was only sporadically showing up. "He finally lived there in lonely splendor," Johnson wrote in 1967.

Cashup suffered a great indignity on June 4, 1896. Due to his celebrity status, the event got picked up in the regional newspapers, much to his embarrassment. He had been in Oakesdale, enjoying a few drinks in one of the saloons and likely telling big tales to those who had gathered. A few drinks later—well, let's presume it was quite a few drinks later—a scoundrel took advantage of the inebriated, elderly Cashup. "He was drunk in the saloon," reported the Spokane *Spokesman-Review*, "when someone cut his pocket from the outside and took his money. Mr. Davis does not know the exact amount, but says it was only a few dollars of silver." The robber must have been watching the rich old man for some time to even know where he was putting this money. This was a brazen act in a small town where everyone knew everyone, except for those just passing through. "Cash-up Davis Was Robbed," blared the headline. Readers who knew Cashup must have thought how sad it was that after losing his wife, followed by much of his hotel business, now someone had picked his pocket.

Tragically, his family's fate worsened. Just eighteen days later, on a sunny Monday morning, June 22, 1896, Cashup, while helping one of his sons poison squirrels (so they wouldn't chew on the hotel's wooden structure), apparently ingested the poison.

A yellowed family clipping from an unknown newspaper reports it this way: "As he went around a bend and from the sight of his son, the latter thought he heard his father groan, but as this was not uncommon, he paid little attention to it. Later, however, he thought he heard a call, and becoming alarmed, proceeded at once to the house. He found his father lying on a cot, apparently suffering great agony. Becoming frightened he leaped upon a horse and hastily rode to a neighbor's house to summon aid. When he and several others returned shortly after, Mr. Davis was dead. At age eighty-one he died alone, in the remarkable building that climaxed his remarkable career."

The details of his death varied somewhat in different newspapers. One reported that Cashup's son never saw what happened, but the teenager hired as a helper found Cashup inside on a couch going into spasms before running to the neighbors for help.

Either way, Cashup was gone. News of his death rifled through newspapers far and wide across the nation. "Cash-up Davis Dead," read the headline in the *Spokesman-Review*, by now the dominant newspaper in the region. "He was in his usual health," it read. He "was one of the oldest and most eccentric pioneers in this country . . . [Cashup had] made the butte his religion and was always 'at home' to visitors who came to view his possessions." "Cashup Cashed In," said a tasteless headline in the *Minneapolis Journal*. In a front-page account, the *Garfield Enterprise* reported that "Cashup Davis, the owner of Steptoe butte and the man who expended much money and energy in making it an inland resort, died alone and unattended on the summit of that historic peak last Monday."

Other reports and obituaries focused on his unique character and the tragedy of his final years: "For years, the little quaint old man, full of eccentricities, has been constantly there to receive visitors."

"Cashup Davis was an eccentric man but of great force of character. He was well educated, of wide reading and of extreme mental capacity."

"Davis lived his last years, friendless and alone, in the magnificent palace he had built."

"Triumph and tragedy of Cashup Davis' famed hotel of pioneer days," wrote historian and author Richard Scheuerman. "Davis became a solitary figure in his Palouse Country castle, the forlorn image of a man devoted to a plan that was impractical."

CASH-UP DAVIS DEAD

One of the Oldest and Most Eccentric Men of the Country.

OWNED STEPTOE BUTTE

Here a Quarter of a Century Ago and Took Part in the Indian Wars.

Oakesdale, Wash., June 22. — "Cashup" Davis died at his home this morning at 9:30 o'clock very unexpectedly. He was in his usual health and had gone with his hired man to help poison squirrels, and when he came home he seemed out of breath and thought he would lie down. He did so, and died immediately.

"Cashup" Davis was one of the oldest and most eccentric pioneers in this country. He came here a quarter of a century ago and was in the Indian wars at that time. He pre-empted Steptoe butte years ago and thought it would be his fortune in his old age. He had since that time made the butte his religion and was always "at home" to visitors who came to view his possessions. In the summer season people came from far and near to Steptoe butte to "view the landscape o'er." Mr. Davis leaves a wife and several sons, the latter being grown men.

The news of Cashup's death in the *Spokesman-Review*, June 24, 1896. From Newspapers.com.

Cashup's younger brother Sivyer, despite their estrangement, knew Cashup in a way no one else did. In the letter he wrote to the family after Mary Ann's death, he expressed concern about the impact her passing would have on Cashup. "How is his health and how is he getting along now[?] [D]oes he stay on the Butte in the Summer time[?]" He wondered, "whether having his wife taken away from him at his age has made any serious inroads to his health."

He described Cashup in a stream-of-consciousness way:

Cashup Davis's funeral procession from the Davis schoolhouse, 1896. Steptoe Butte and the hotel are visible in the background. From the Washington State Archives.

I was with him so many years in his young days and have seen him sometimes in places that it would of taken the most heroic person to of got out of it but he did every time but always done it honorable then he has a big heart when he has the means so I have always thought a good deal of him but him and I have not seen alike a great many times but I always liked a big hearted man and he was one in all the troubles I have seen him in I have seen him when two men have been fighting and the largest man was abusing the poor little fellow terribly I have seen him step out of the crowd and took the little one . . . then he had to fight the large man as heavy again as he was but he always whipped his man. I never knew him [to] fail.

Those are powerful words: I never knew him to fail. Cashup, too, never knew himself to fail.

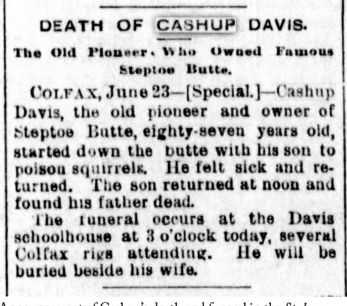

DEATH OF CASHUP DAVIS.

The Old Pioneer, Who Owned Famous Steptoe Butte.

COLFAX, June 23—[Special.]—Cashup Davis, the old pioneer and owner of Steptoe Butte, eighty-seven years old, started down the butte with his son to poison squirrels. He felt sick and returned. The son returned at noon and found his father dead.

The funeral occurs at the Davis schoolhouse at 3 o'clock today, several Colfax rigs attending. He will be buried beside his wife.

Announcement of Cashup's death and funeral in the *Spokane Chronicle*, June 23, 1896. From Newspapers.com.

His funeral service at the Davis schoolhouse near the butte was packed with friends, family, neighbors, admirers—maybe even a few detractors. Reverend Todd, the family friend and occasional guest at the hotel who had delivered Mary Ann's sermon less than nineteen months before, delivered one for Cashup too.

The funeral procession was captured in one of the more well-known pioneer-era photos of the Palouse. It is the only photograph of the funeral known to exist. In the distance, a long line of mourners approach what is believed to be the Davis schoolhouse. The funeral procession was one of the biggest and most elaborate the region had seen. Riding the carriage with another man, perhaps his son Ed, in the driver's platform, Reverend Todd leads the mourners, as two dark-colored horses pull a regal hearse adorned with lanterns and ornaments and full windows on each side. More than a dozen carriages and horses stretch out far behind, a measured cadence nearing Cashup's final resting spot.

The funeral record indicates Cashup's son Edward and "Frank" Davis ordered the arrangements, including an embellished casket draped in black cloth. Cost: $75—a good sum in 1896. It took six months for $50 to be paid toward the bill and another four months to pay off the remainder. The slow remittance may have been a sign of financial troubles to come in the wake of Cashup's death.

Cashup was so in love with the butte that he was quite serious about his pronounced desire to be buried on its peak. "He dug his own grave and left the spade standing beside it. He often pointed this out to friends, stressing his intention." Cashup told people he wanted that burial site to be a monument, a "tomb for himself which was to have been built of massive masonry. Here he wished to have his body buried in a standing position." Not out of ego, really, but to commemorate the success of the hotel's construction for history. Other accounts suggest he intended the hotel itself as "a kind of monument to his memory when he was gone."

OK, maybe his ego was involved.

After he died, his family decided against his wishes, likely for a variety of reasons. For example, it might be difficult to sell land with a grave marker on it. And perhaps they did not like the idea of their parents being buried separately. Instead, the day after he died, they buried him next to Mary Ann in Bethel Cemetery on Tennessee Flats, where his soul could have a grand view in perpetuity of that glorious peak of his. Cashup and Mary Ann were together again, marked by the tallest, grandest tombstone in the cemetery. "The ironic but sadly true to life finish of Cashup's chapter; his death, alone and unattended in the ruin of his greatest dream," wrote Johnson.

Cashup Quietly Piled Up Debt

Cashup faced withering criticism from his contemporaries for investing in the hotel on Steptoe Butte—an outlandish project that risked his fortune. The venture ultimately exemplifies the pros and cons inherent in all such gambles: Chasing a dream often attracts critics, which you have to learn to ignore. Essentially, the road to realizing a dream is littered with caveats.

While researching my great-grandfather's life, I found that when Cashup was raising money to buy Steptoe Butte and to pay the construction costs of the road and hotel, he borrowed money and put up his home, stage stop, and farmland as collateral. Yes, the man known for using cash only went into debt to build and run his dream hotel.

Part of the story of Cashup's hotel financing is found in the land abstract for Cashup and Mary Ann's properties. A land abstract is a written record of all legal transactions concerning a given piece of property, a document common for farms in that era that owners leveraged to finance the next crop. The paperwork was discovered in 2021 by Rusty McGuire, the adult son of Lee and Linda McGuire, who live on Cashup's former property. When the legal actions chronicled in the abstract are placed in a timeline of Cashup's final months, a disturbing story reveals itself. Its tight chronology:

January 1, 1896. The very day Sivyer writes that heartfelt letter about Mary Ann, expressing concern about Cashup's well-being, the New England Mortgage Company of Connecticut begins foreclosure proceedings in court to take Cashup's home, stage stop, and farmland. The property under litigation was separate from the butte and the hotel but was still the emotional heart and soul of the family.

February 17, 1896. The New England Mortgage Company also seeks to seize the estate of Mary Ann. There is no evidence in the abstract indicating that the family fought against it.

April 2, 1896. A Whitman County Superior Court judge orders Cashup and his family to pay $8,572.80 in a default judgment. The judge orders Whitman County Sheriff John Lathrum to sell the property at a public auction on the courthouse steps in Colfax in front of the community that so admires Cashup and whose attention Cashup so enjoys.

May 2, 1896. After weeks of enduring humiliating (but legally required) advertising notices in the *Colfax Gazette*, Cashup sells his land to satisfy the debt he could not cover.

June 4, 1896. Cashup visits the bar in Oakesdale and gets drunk and is robbed. The *Spokesman-Review* reports that Cashup tried to brush it off.

June 15, 1896. Judge E. E. Sullivan affirms the sale of the Davis family home, stage stop, and farmland. Even though the children are adults who live in their own homes, losing the Davis home is devastating. It is sold for the amount owed. "'The Valley at Cashup' is foreclosed for mortgage," wrote Eckhart in her chronicle.

June 20, 1896. Cashup dies alone in his hotel after setting out poison to exterminate squirrels on top of Steptoe Butte.

Public health data for this period shows that in 1896, the most common method of suicide was poison. The types of poisons used were those "available on the farm, where strychnine, cyanide and arsenic were used against rabbits and other pests." How likely is it that accidentally inhaling poisonous fumes outdoors can be lethal? Or, if someone dies from ingesting a pest poison, how likely is it that the death was intentional?

Order of sale for the James "Cashup" Davis property, issued by the Superior Court of the state of Washington to the Whitman County sheriff, April 2, 1896. From Whitman County Abstracts, courtesy of Rusty McGuire

Cashup met six of the eight leading risk factors for suicide, as found in present-day studies:

1. Male
2. Caucasian
3. Elderly
4. Divorced (before Mary Ann's death, the two were estranged)
5. Time of year (spring or summer season)
6. Newly unemployed (Cashup had lost the family home, stage stop, and farmland just five days prior to his death; and, of course, his hotel business was failing)

We will never know with certainty whether Cashup took his own life. After reviewing the events of the last six months of his life, I think it likely he intentionally poisoned himself. He was a proud, stubborn man. He had always succeeded in life; he had recently lost his wife and, when his business failed catastrophically, the additional setback was likely too much to bear.

During those five days between Judge Sullivan's final order and his death, Cashup must have walked the halls in utter anguish. I can only imagine how devastated he felt. I wonder whether those close to him suspected or knew he took his life but, in the unspoken customs of the era, kept it a secret.

Strangely, this news does not change my view of Cashup. In fact, it underscores my respect for him because his drive for success was so enormous. But at this point our story turns into a cautionary tale—that chasing your dreams and finding the determination to ignore critics comes with a price. Or to realize that success is not the end-all be-all. For what other goals do you reach once you've achieved them? Must you continue to succeed to be known as a success? And what is "success" anyway; how does one define it? Cashup got his hotel built. That was an enormous achievement, though it ultimately failed. Despite the way things worked out at the end of his life, I believe that Cashup, the person, was not a failure.

"His arduous labor ended in serious depletion of his available assets," wrote S. C. Roberts, and "his estate afforded but meager bequests to his heirs." After his death, the family still had to make payments on the hotel. His family decided to keep the hotel operating. Cashup's son Frank, at the age of thirty-nine, took on the operation. He promoted the hotel and advertised the telescope again: 25 cents per look. "The huge telescope is in position and the hotel has been thoroughly repaired," claimed an article in the *Colfax Gazette* on July 20, 1900.

It didn't work, however. The hotel doors shut permanently in 1900 or 1901. With the family unable to make payments on the remaining debt, the hotel and 160 acres at the summit of Steptoe Butte "was sold for the mortgage on it." Inevitable, but sad indeed. "To satisfy a judgement amounting, with attorney's fees, to nearly $2000, obtained by the Canadian & American Mortgage company of London, Steptoe butte, the historic landmark of Whitman County, is to be sold at sheriff's sale on Saturday, April 26," reported the *Colfax Gazette* on April 4. "Since the death of Mr. Davis the property has not been kept up and today bears evidence of the ravages of time and neglect . . . [I]t is hoped that [the] change of ownership may result in its preservation and reopening as a resort."

Following the default and sale at auction, one of the railroad companies got the property and announced plans to renovate and re-open the hotel. It is unclear whether the hotel ever actually re-opened under railroad ownership, but they did produce marketing materials, including a 1904 illustration postcard depicting the hotel.

During his life, Cashup's fiery ambition and vision came between him and his family, including Mary Ann and several of the older children who lived nearby. "He was determined to a fault." All his life, he had been a powerful, domineering figure in his family. After his death, that legacy continued, but in a different way—the family was saddled with debt. Unquestionably, it caused tension in the family—even anger at their famous father—before and after his death, although no explicit accounts record such sentiments. Mary Ann even submitted a declaration in court, found in the abstract, that anyone considering loaning Cashup money using their land as collateral needed to get her permission as a co-owner.

When I sat for an on-camera interview with Randall Johnson, the amateur historian, in 2000, he told me that he actually spoke to Cashup's children about the man's domineering ways. "I never talked to any of them who had anything real negative to say about him. I think that some of them thought they had been taken advantage of by him. But this was not unusual either [in that era]. The patriarch was considered to be the boss of the kids, so I wouldn't really know how to separate that. But all I'm sure of is that he was a colorful, forceful, and almost unbelievable character in the settling of the early West."

In 1888, the number of white settlers in eastern Washington was still sparse. Getting up to the top of the butte was difficult without the transportation options available a short time later. Indeed, cars came to the Palouse within ten years. One newspaper article eschewed the idea that the hotel was one hundred years ahead of its time, suggesting it was only forty years too soon. My view, however, is that Cashup's hotel would not succeed even today because it is too remote, too far from an airport, has too little space at the summit, and still has no water.

"The hotel's big advantage—its position at the pinnacle—was also its downfall. It was simply too hard to get to," wrote Jim Kershner in a March 26, 2006, remembrance in the *Spokesman-Review.*

The Spokane and Inland Company, the railroad that owned the land around the butte, reacquired the summit and the old building and announced plans in 1908 to restore and reopen the hotel. "An automobile road leading to the summit is now under construction, and by next year parties may go there to spend the day." But the project never moved forward. The hotel was abandoned. Critters and spider webs had their way. Gradually, it was robbed of its elaborate wood trim. The window glass deteriorated. After countless squalls and gales and blusters, the incessant forces of the wind turned the walls sullen and gray. The excitement and the joy, the clatter and the warmth, became a part of the past. "The people are gone," wrote Johnson in his unpublished notes, "[only] the breeze through the bunchgrass on the solitary butte makes the words and music."

In his final days, walking the dark hallways alone, without friends, without Mary Ann, without most of his family, without guests coming to his hotel, Cashup may have felt like a failure, like the worth of his life had vanished, that what he worked so hard to achieve was all for not.

His greatest achievement was also his greatest failure. Or so he may have thought. The truth Cashup did not see at the time was about to be revealed to everyone. It would be Cashup's true worth.

Visitors to the hotel, 1902. From the Joe Wagner family.

The shuttered hotel hosts a man seated on the roof, 1903.

Postcard produced to promote the hotel on Steptoe Butte, 1904. Image courtesy of Whitman County Rural Heritage.

James "Cashup" Davis, undated photo. From the Davis family.

TWELVE

CASHUP'S GREATEST ACHIEVEMENT AND GREATEST FAILURE

"The most important things in life are intangible."

THOM HARTMANN

IN 2020, THE OCTOBER WIND at the summit of Steptoe Butte is blowing on this day just as it has since Cashup's time here 125 years ago. It is downright cold. Instead of a magnificent hotel sitting atop this incredible viewpoint, dozens of people have gathered to honor Cashup. Everyone here has something in common.

Cashup's legacy was never his hotel, or the stage stop, or his farm, or his fame. Or his money, while he had it. The real legacy he left behind is the inspiration to chase your dreams. Risk and reward were the tenets of his life. Never let the cynics deter you. Yet be aware of this cautionary tale. Such lessons are available to anyone then and now—even to the readers of this book. And no one knows this better, no one manifests that inspiration more directly than the scores of people mingling at the summit: They are Cashup Davis's descendants, the key part of his legacy he overlooked, even while his family was right under his nose. Cashup's fierce desire for success, while admirable, blinded him to the intangible value of a family whom he may not have even realized he was inspiring.

Heck, you don't need to be a member of the family to be inspired by Cashup and Mary Ann. Their inspiration is there for the taking, by anyone, anywhere, at any time. Any time someone tells you that you can't achieve your dream, remember Cashup.

"To be 74 years old and walk up this butte and actually fulfill a dream that he had and bring it to fruition, even though in the end he failed, I feel like he was very successful in completing his dreams," says Jackie Davis at the summit gathering. It is a common notion among those who know the real story of Cashup Davis. Success is not, as he thought, the achievements. Instead, it is the act of achieving—indeed, it is the desire to act—and how that action affects the people closest to you. It is all about the journey. "I think he was a visionary," says Jackie. "He had dreams and goals that were his own. I think he was amazing for fulfilling most of his dreams even when people were telling him they were ridiculous."

Imagine the story of Cashup's life had he listened to all those people who told him, "Don't leave school to travel with the Captain," "Don't leave England for America," "Don't leave New York for the West," "Don't give up your farmland in Wisconsin, Iowa, or Oregon for uncertain land claims in an unknown region," "Don't live among Native Americans who might be furious at white settlers," "Do not spend your life's earnings to buy Steptoe Butte and, for God's sake, do not build a hotel on the summit!" Even with the closing of the hotel, Cashup's life was a success, not because of what he did but because of who he was and how he inspires others.

The scores of Davis family members gathered at the summit and shared smiles, laughs, hugs, photos, chatter, stories, and pride. Through the generations, the descendants of Cashup and Mary Ann now bear many different family names, branching off into last names like Martin, Williams, Lindley, Rupp, and so many more. I invited the Davis descendants to this gathering to honor the inspiration of Cashup and Mary Ann and to announce the Gordon Davis Family Endowment of the Cashup Davis Dean of Washington State University's College of Agricultural, Human, and Natural Resource Sciences (CAHNRS). This deanship honors Cashup in perpetuity and is fittingly the first of its kind at any university or college of agricultural science in the nation. And later that day, more than a hundred Davis family members gathered on the WSU campus in Pullman to thank ol' Cashup. It is a proud day for all the Cashup descendants and, importantly, anyone else inspired by him.

I told the assembled crowd: "Cashup was a risk taker." That is it, in a nutshell. That is the nugget that so many others can learn from this wily pioneer. Whether it is in one's professional endeavors or personal life, big or small, tangible or intangible, taking a risk is living life like Cashup. It might be starting a business, or being a better person, parent, spouse, friend. Putting yourself outside your comfort zone is living the Cashup life. Yet be aware that, in any endeavor you undertake, skill must go hand in hand with determination. One cannot work to become a successful singer without a good voice, or become a successful businessperson without the skill set to work with others. So, ignore the naysayers, but make darned sure you have the talent and skills you need.

And the life lesson is clear: Our success in life is not measured by tangible objects but rather by how we touch lives, inspire hearts and minds, and create happiness for others in perpetuity.

Charley Bought It Back

The family was presumably devastated when the family home, ranch, stage stop, outbuildings, and farmland were foreclosed and lost during Cashup's final days. As a testament to the tenacity Cashup and Mary Ann had imbued in their family, something extraordinary happened just six years later. Charley Davis, Cashup's youngest son and my grandfather, managed to save up

Eight of Cashup and Mary Ann's eleven children at the Davis family reunion in 1911. Front row: William, Henry, Charles, and John; Back row: Laura (married name Littell), Frances (McMeekin), Mary Ann (Martin), and Amy Charlotte (Lindley). From the collection of Jim Martin, restored.

$5,259 and, on November 6, 1902, he bought back 300 acres of the family farm near the base of Steptoe Butte, including the family home and the historic stage stop itself. Oh, how he must have felt. It is also the spot where nearly all of Cashup and Mary Ann's children and grandchildren reunited on July 30, 1911. The ruins of Cashup's hotel had burned to the ground four months earlier, in a mysterious nighttime fire. More than 60 members of Cashup and Mary Ann's family—their children, grandchildren, and extended families—gathered for the first Davis family reunion. "The day was perfect for such a gathering," reported the *Colfax Gazette* a few days later. The Palouse weather had hovered in the upper 90s that week. "And the picnic dinner was served under the trees which were set out long ago by the paternal ancestor of the large family."

Among the photographs from that day is one of my proud grandfather hosting the clan. Another photo from the event shows eight of the 11 adult children of Cashup and Mary Ann sitting in two rows: William, Laura (Littell), Frances or "Fanny" (McMeekin), Henry, John, Mary Ann (Martin), and the two youngest, Charlotte "Lottie" (Lindley) and my grandfather Charley. Ferd was not able to attend because he was traveling in California, and James was living back east. Clarence was the only sibling who had died, having succumbed just 15 months earlier at age 50, in Colfax. It is unclear how he died but he had fought alcohol abuse for some time.

Another photo from that 1911 family reunion shows the entire gathering in the shade of trees that had grown so much larger and bigger than when travelers and revelers had sat beneath them years earlier. Photographs of the era almost always show serious, non-smiling faces posing for the large cameras they had back then. But this photo is different. It includes people smiling, laughing, doing antics—even young women and men arm in arm with mischievous expressions. An 18-month-old toddler in that photo is my dad Aubrey, son of Charley. Dad told me he was born on the second floor of the stage stop. I am stunned to have this unique link to Cashup's history.

***

The old Territorial Road had been replaced by a better road in the early 1900s, but its route was moved slightly and sliced the old farm in half. The paved state highway was still a few decades away.

Several years after the reunion, Charley built a beautiful home a few yards away from the stage stop, where he and his wife Grace—my grandmother—raised their family. The cistern in the basement displays the initials "CJ" that I am sure my grandfather proudly placed there. When the Great Depression hit in 1930, crop prices fell by 60 percent and unemployment rose to 23 percent.

In 1931, frantic for new sources of income, my grandfather hired architects to draw up plans for renovating and expanding the old stage stop into a restaurant and hotel. Using the Cashup ambition, they had hoped to bring back the magic and make new memories. But the length of the Depression stopped everything. The blueprints still exist, but the plans were never carried out.

Then circumstances got really bad for Charley and Grace. To get cash to feed their family, they had to mortgage their property to a man named Earl Berry. Berry would hold the deed until they paid him back, presumably with interest. To help make the payments, my dad, who was then twenty-six, and his younger brother Chuck, twenty-four, unloaded train loads of coal, and hauled 135-pound wheat sacks from the fields to the granary for 5 cents per sack. Despite their efforts, Berry kept the land, the stage stop, and the new house. Grace wrote in a letter: "[My husband] lost it all in the depression of 29-33 and was forced to sell for what was against it . . . [Our family] is living in a modest home at Malden, Wash. But he feels he added his bit to the community at Cashup in the form of a modern dwelling that will always be known as the Charley Davis place."

Grandpa Charley died in 1936. My dad and Uncle Chuck were bitter their whole lives over that bad deal and never had a good thing to say about Earl Berry.

In the 1980s, Berry sold the home and land to Lee and Linda McGuire, friends of our family whose ancestors had married into the Davis family. They live there to this day, telling Cashup stories to friends, occasionally finding artifacts, and acknowledging the visitors who want to look at the land Cashup made famous. My dad and Uncle Chuck moved to Deer Park, a farming community north of Spokane, where they did very well and where my life was shaped on the family dairy farm, named the best in the state in 1964.

Like Charley, many of Cashup and Mary Ann's children rose to become leaders of their community. Many stayed on the

Palouse, married into other pioneer families, navigated the ups and downs to earn their own wealth, and contributed to their communities. Among them were a postmaster, a bank president, and a judge. Family members helped to bring in telephone lines, invented and patented farming equipment, and advanced agriculture. Their pride in Cashup and Mary Ann, the tough father and the strong mother, was carried on through the later generations.

The descendants do have a leg up on others. Many are imbued with those audacious Cashup genes that gave him fortitude and work ethic to achieve so much. Here are just two examples: My nephew Dave Davis became an airline captain with Southwest Airlines. Cousin Duane Mars Davis became an internationally acclaimed poet in the 1960s and was honored personally by the Kennedy family for his poem about the president. And in so many other ways, in business, in family, civic leadership, and an extraordinary legacy in agriculture, Cashup descendants often exhibited his spirit.

Newspaper accounts of Cashup became less frequent over the years. With each, the reporter had to provide more explanation of who Cashup was, as he was no longer a household name. He was slipping out of the cultural memory. The railroad station near Cashup's old stage stop turned into the tiny town of Cashup, marked to this day by a smattering of buildings, the familiar green highway sign "Cashup" and emblazoned on the side of a tall grain elevator is the name "Cashup."

As certain as time itself, Cashup's children began to perish too. Two of the siblings, Ferd and Frances, died the same day in an extraordinary, heartbreaking story. It unfolded this way: On April 12, 1924, Ferd died in Spokane of a heart attack. Later that day, Frances' family arrived at her house for their daily visit, planning not to tell her yet about Ferd's death to spare her the shock. But no one had told Frances' four-year-old grandnephew George Martin to stay quiet. When they arrived at Frances' house, the little boy, who had been listening to the adults talk about it, jumped out of the car and dashed to the porch where Frances was waiting. He blurted out, "Uncle Ferd is dead!" Hearing the news that her closest sibling had passed, Frances fell into an emotional turmoil, saying something like, "Well then, I have nothing to live for and will not try," according to family papers. She died a half hour later while lying on her bed.

"My dad never forgot this day," says Jim Martin, "feeling he was responsible for her death. When he spoke of this moment in time, it was clear that it was etched in his mind...his voice would quiver with emotions and it was tough for the words to come out. A burden he carried his whole life."

Both Ferd and Frances had lived long, successful lives of notable wealth. The Cashup work ethic endured. When Henry "Ed" Davis died in 1926, he still had a list of things to do, his family wrote. The family would literally refill the toothpaste tubes rather than throw them away.

Historian S. C. Roberts described Cashup's inspiration to family and friends: "a priceless heritage of his family is shared by a wide circle of contemporary pioneer friends and neighbors who cannot forget their eccentric but kindly fellow citizen, Cashup Davis." And he continued: "it is a pleasure to record the fact that they [Cashup's heirs] all are well to do and in comfortable circumstances."

In 1919, three Palouse pioneers—George H. McCroskey, Dr. E. Maguire, and J. S. Klemgard—wanted to reflect on Cashup. They climbed to the summit of Steptoe Butte, looked at Cashup's view, honored him, then descended and rested at the old stage stop. Karl Allen was there to chronicle the whole thing for his newspaper and snap a few photos. They agreed Cashup was the Palouse's most noteworthy pioneer, more responsible for making the world aware of the Palouse than anyone else. Allen described the "weathered" stage stop: "moss covered and decayed, it is pointed out to the hundreds of tourists as one of Whitman

Sharon Williams, great-great-grand-daughter of Cashup and Mary Ann, holds a pitcher from the hotel. Photograph by Jeff Burnside.

A celery holder from Cashup's hotel. Photograph by Jeff Burnside.

county's points of interest and is treasured by early day settlers as the scene of their youthful frolics" whose "children's children now point to the relic of pioneer days with interest and pride." He noted that Charley owned it later, built his fine home nearby, "and within its walls are carefully preserved scores of relics of the early days."

At least nine items once owned by Cashup and featured in the hotel or stage stop are still held dear by his descendants. Like any historic icon, they are physical representations of the past:

- The telescope from the hotel
- His top hat
- His bed
- A clock
- A wooden cash register (whereabouts now unknown)
- A blue and white platter

A British serving platter used in Cashup's hotel now owned by family descendant Linda Banken. Photograph by Jeff Burnside.

- An ornate glass water pitcher
- A glass celery holder
- A kerosene lamp
- And, of course, a handful of square nails indicative of the period. The lucky hand and sharp eye can still find them at the summit, buried beneath the dirt.

Many of the family items, letters, photos, and research were compiled by Julia Davis Eckhart, granddaughter of Cashup and daughter of Henry "Ed" Davis who died in the 1960s. We have cited Julia's work many times in this book because she made it her mission to gather the history to hand off to descendants who have since supplemented those handwritten notes. "She was a big woman," laughs Donna Gwinn, Julia's granddaughter. "She loved to tell stories and laugh." She dutifully took photos of headstones so the family would remember.

To this day, homesteading families across the Palouse are memorialized by roads named after them, crisscrossing the hills and connecting family farmhouse with family farmhouse. Among them is a Cashup Avenue and a Davis Avenue. Many of the families named on the green road signs continue to farm the land 140 years or more after homesteading. Virgil McCroskey used part of his fortune to buy 40 acres at the summit of Steptoe Butte that Cashup had once owned. In August 1946, McCroskey donated his land to the state of Washington in exchange for turning it into a park and preserving it forever. (McCroskey also bought and donated a large swath of magnificent land a few miles east in Idaho as a park named after his mother.) A new paved road circling and climbing the butte was built, replacing the difficult switchback road Cashup and his team had built by hand. Where the hotel once stood are now public bathrooms and a utility building to support a collection of massive antennas facilitating electronic communication

Gordon Davis (left) contemplates the cistern location on Steptoe Butte with Jim Martin and Gordon's grandson Reese Rodriguez. Photograph by Jeff Burnside.

across the Palouse (while creating an eyesore that can be seen for miles in every direction).

In the middle of the paved parking lot at the top is a depression that is slowly deepening. Jim Martin, knowledgeable of the Cashup story, believes it is the site of the 35-foot-deep cistern built by Cashup's team in hopes of providing water to the hotel.

When the remains of the hotel were demolished after the fire, some of the rubble was likely tossed into the cistern. As park officials discuss new paving at the summit, some eagerly clamor to open up the cistern and dig out relics of the old hotel that may be waiting to be discovered.

To the side of the summit is a kiosk telling the geologic history of the butte and discussing Virgil McCroskey's generosity, but it makes only a brief mention of Cashup Davis. A growing cadre of Cashup Davis fans feel he deserves much more recognition than that. I intend to evaluate options of what could be done to preserve his legacy on top of Steptoe Butte.

And what of the long-standing rumor that two teenage boys were seen outside the hotel as it began to burn? It turns out to be true. But there was a twist to that story. Some folks peddling gossip believe the hotel in its later years was the scene of ill repute, despite absolutely no evidence, and claim the boys were hired to burn the hotel to get rid of that problem. But this cannot be true because the fire happened a full decade after the hotel was abandoned and left to deteriorate.

Another theory suggests landowner Robert Burns might have been the culprit. He was the neighbor who had orchards of apples, apricots, plums, peaches, and pears as well as cattle on the northern access to the summit of the butte. After the hotel was abandoned around 1902 and allowed to deteriorate, curious visitors kept going to the top to see the buildings. After the road became impassible, many climbed it on foot. The story goes they would open one of Burns' gates to get to the summit and sometimes leave it open, allowing Burns' cows to get out. Could it be that Burns wanted to deter climbing to the summit by removing the temptation of the hotel? Family murmurs say Burns paid the two kids to burn it down. If true, his idea yielded results.

A less nefarious theory is that two kids were simply doing what kids do: playing with fire. A few sparks would have been all that was needed to start the conflagration.

Paul T. Bockmier was an elderly man in 1968 when he wrote a curious letter to Johnson. Bockmier had grown up in the town of Palouse and remembers visiting the hotel as a kid. In his letter he recalls that his father, Paul Sr., a pioneer who had arrived in the area just before the hotel opened, told his son about Cashup's telescope. "My Dad often told of the country he could see when he looked thru the telescope," he wrote. "I knew one of the boys who was reported to have started the fire." Bockmier, not wanting to foist such guilt and burden on his acquaintance, never names him.

We came close to learning the names during an extraordinary death bed phone call. Remember the four-year-old George Martin who blurted out to his grandmother that her brother had just passed away? Much later in life, according to his son Jim, he got a phone call that made him sit down. An elderly man was on the line, saying he was in a hospital bed and he needed to get something off his chest before he died. He shared that he was one of the boys who set the hotel on fire and that he needed to come clean so he could die in peace.

George, who had dealt with his own guilt his entire life over his great-aunt's death, kept secret the name of the old man on the phone. But my research for this book has finally confirmed the name of the boy. After more than 110 years, multiple members of the family contacted for this book are finally ready to reveal the name: Lawrence Bishop. Lawrence was a teenager in 1911 when, one evening, he and a buddy had climbed Steptoe Butte and started playing with fire. It went horribly out of control. They ran back down the butte to the nearest house, where Lawrence was living with his grandparents, John and Edna Bishop, on the edge of the town of Garfield.

As news of the fire raced throughout the region, the Bishop family went into quiet mode to protect the family name. It was a prominent family full of model citizens, but Lawrence was the black sheep of the family, the little rascal who was always getting into trouble. "My grandmother was extraordinarily scandalized by the whole thing," says Stephen Bishop, "and it scandalized my family for generations." Stephen, a prominent lawyer in Garfield who is now mostly retired, runs the Bishop Orchard and still owns much of the farm where Lawrence and his co-conspirator hid that night. "It was a big deal" to his grandparents. "The kids were goofing off," he explains, "not intending" to burn down the hotel. "As soon as it got started, they skedaddled down the butte to the farmhouse."

Lawrence lived on for years around Garfield without much of anyone outside the family knowing "the big secret," says Stephen. But he also continued to misbehave and struggled with alcohol. After marrying and having several children, he abandoned his family and moved to live with a woman in Creston, British Columbia, where he spent the rest of his life. His children and grandchildren went on to live exemplary lives, one even becoming a war hero in the South Pacific during World War II.

Was it Lawrence who had a change of heart on his death bed to make that phone call confession to George Martin? Stephen believes Lawrence's death was sudden, which would not account for a hospital stay and a phone call. Besides, Stephen does not believe that Lawrence would have had the fortitude or remorse to make such a call. Perhaps that means it was Lawrence's buddy—the one who helped light the fire that night and whose name has been lost with time—who made the guilt-ridden phone call from his death bed.

Cashup's hotel, gone for more than a century, is still touching lives, as are Cashup and Mary Ann, and the many descendants in the Davis family. Through the dreams Cashup chased, he brought happiness, frivolity, optimism, friendship, and hospitality to a pioneer community that, by its nature, was often focused on surviving until the next crop came in or the next round of livestock was sold. His colorful character made the Palouse more interesting and created one of the most treasured stories of the time.

LIFE LESSONS FROM THE MOUNTAINTOP

AS I WROTE AT THE beginning of this book, Cashup is my secret mentor. Let him be yours too. My journey to find out more about Cashup Davis taught me many things. I learned a lot about myself—good and bad, frankly. My life is a continuing pursuit for excellence—just like Cashup's was. And, like Cashup, I often succeed and sometimes fail—but I never give up.

When my grandfather Charley and father Aubrey lost the family farm to Earl Berry in the 1930s, they found strength in adversity. For the first time in his life, my dad had no farmland. It broke his heart. He moved to Spokane and lived there for a few years before leasing 320 acres near Thornton, WA, to farm. My dad was an exemplary farmer. In 1951, he harvested a big crop of wheat, sixty bushels per acre. The yield was so high the landowner bought out my dad's lease for $18,000. With that money, my parents bought a rundown eighty-acre dairy farm in Deer Park, WA, where I grew up and developed my work ethic. So, in my view, if Berry had not taken over our Palouse farm, I might never have had the dairy farm experience that gave me the background to start my own company and succeed later in life. When opportunity knocks, blast right through the door and don't look back.

I am also particularly struck by the following parallels in Cashup's and my life:

DEFINING SUCCESS: How do you define success in your life?

One of the greatest lessons we can learn from Cashup's life is that success can be defined outside of material gains or track records of achievement. Success may already be surrounding you. Cashup kept searching for success, which prevented him from enjoying the achievements he already had: family, being happy with who he was, and acknowledging what he had already accomplished.

VISION: When Cashup envisioned his financial independence

Was it when he was a young man, leading a team of sixty adults in engineering the tunnel through the cliffs of England, that Cashup decided to seek financial independence? Was it the moment Mary Ann made him stop his attempt to move the family from the Palouse to Canada? Was it when he opened the stage stop and hosted crowds until dawn? Or on the opening day of the hotel? I had the vision at age twenty-six to achieve financial independence by age fifty. I knew I needed one idea. I found that idea at age thirty-six and established the independence I sought at age sixty; now, at age seventy-seven, I look back, knowing it has been a rewarding journey. Along the way my efforts have helped educate millions of Career Technical Education (CTE) students—a much bigger reward than any material windfall.

CHASE YOUR DREAMS: Everyone told Cashup he was crazy to build his hotel

In April 2001, I risked it all to make a fundamental pivot with my modest company. Like a poker game, I moved all my chips into play: I liquidated my retirement and 401k investment accounts, withdrew my savings, sold our home to employ the equity if needed, rented a smaller place, and borrowed $2.1 million. My company, CEV Multimedia, which had been producing supplementary education materials, shifted to publishing full courses. I made this move after learning about a multibillion-dollar fund in Texas for purchasing instructional materials for schools. In forty-eight hours, I had changed our company's vision.

Almost everyone thought I was crazy. All but five of my employees quit, most likely reasoning that I did not possess the wherewithal to make the transition. But we prevailed. The company's first major contract for $9.3 million was wired to us October 20, 2005, at 7:57 a.m.—just in time to make payments on the loan, fund the company's operation, and care for my family. Was it a long shot? Yes. Was I all in? Absolutely. With 12.5% of my genes from Cashup, I had a secret weapon. I was not scared and I was absolutely not going to fail.

Today, my company—now called iCEV Multimedia—is the nation's leading provider of instructional materials for CTE teachers across the United States and internationally. Sales tripled in 2020, with more growth in subsequent years. Many of Cashup's keys to success—risk taking, determination, tenacity—have been woven into the company for the past forty years. I believe that Cashup would be proud of what we built before selling it in December 2021.

FOCUS: When Cashup was raising funds for his hotel

I can only imagine what Cashup experienced when raising capital for his vision of a grand hotel in the 1880s. To start my business at age forty-two, I made proposals to three banks. Two banks said no, but one said yes! My first loan was for $50,000. My last one in 2016 was for $3,750,000. It is very tough to be the man in the mirror with no one else to pay off the debt if you fail. Cashup knew that too.

PERSEVERENCE: Cashup stopped at nothing to become world class

His vision was unique and world class—he had a commitment to a superior level of quality and to stay competitive with anyone anywhere. In 1998, we made it a goal to become world class at what we were doing at CEV Multimedia. We reached that level in 2017. If one pursues excellence day-to-day, guess what? Excellence can be attained. To quote Aristotle, we are what we repeatedly do. Excellence, then, is not an act but a habit. Cashup's vision for a hotel was world class. From 1888 to about 1891, the hotel was, in fact, world class.

FLEXIBILITY: Trains killed the stage stop

Cashup's stage stop went out of business after the train came in and killed the stagecoach. Because he was willing to adapt to change, he developed his next venture: the hotel. In the 1930s, my dad showed similar character, by trading in his team of horses and mules for a motorized tractor. I experienced the need for flexibility throughout my career building CEV—at inception by bringing experts to the classroom via a TV screen, then moving to DVDs and making a big gamble to put our platform online in the early 2000s. If I had remained inflexible, the times would have passed us, and so would have the opportunity to impact CTE education on a global scale. Like Cashup and my dad, I prefer to be on the forefront of change. These three transformational moments all occurred in one family, over each generational lifetime, courtesy of our ability to be flexible, change with the times, and endure the risks that might accrue.

ADAPTABILITY: When Cashup put his stage-stop debt up for sale at 50%

A wise man suggested "50% of something is better than 100% of nothing." Wise, indeed. It worked, and likewise, I assume Cashup's 50%-off plan worked too.

LOVE: Tension in Cashup's family

When Cashup became too focused on personal achievement, it caused tension in his family—something that impacts all driven people. I have worked hard to avoid that. But not perfectly. Rather than conduct my affairs in a domineering way as Cashup did, I have generally sought input from others, so my final decision is based on the contribution of others I respect. I have found I get it right more often than not. In business, however, if you're right 100% of the time, you're not taking enough chances. My wife Joyce is my rock and my best friend and I love her deeply. She questions some of my bad ideas; no doubt Mary Ann voted no to many of Cashup's ideas as well.

Yet I have tension in other parts of my family, and it causes me great sadness and frustration. I am so deeply proud of my kids and grandkids. Family is too important and life too short. Love your family.

OPTIMISM: Both dangerous and great

Cashup's irrepressible optimism convinced him that, after the stage stop closed, he could build a new, even grander venue. As we know, that strategy worked for a few years before the business died a slow death, for reasons clear to everyone except Cashup. One of his strengths ironically became a weakness—his positive approach blinded and misled him, which is why such optimism, while essential, can also be a liability. This makes me think of the origin of my self-confidence and optimism, as I nearly always think a glass is 90% full, while others, including my wife, children, and employees, prudently think it is less full. Their thinking is wiser, actually. Sometimes, assuming that a glass is 90% full is not practical and makes zero sense. Nevertheless, I prefer making all my mistakes by being too aggressive: history indicates the same was true for Cashup.

KINDNESS: Never lose sight of what's right

Despite his drive and domineering ways, Cashup showed kindness to people and to animals. And his children carried that generosity down through the generations to my aunts and uncles and parents, to me, and then to my children and grandchildren. Kindness is goodness. My father always taught me that a good deal means both sides are happy—not just your side—even if it means backing off a little. This approach has served me well in my academic and business careers, through thousands of interactions with colleagues, bank officers, mentors, employees, teachers, schools, customers, and Sigma Chi fraternity brothers of different temperaments, talents, and convictions. With what I have learned about Cashup, I am sure my dad got that trait from him. It has served me well in my life also.

BALANCE: It's okay to work hard and play hard

Now, here is a shared trait if ever there was one. I feel my philosophy of "it's okay to work hard and play hard" came partially from Cashup. We both love to bring people together: Cashup at his stage stop and hotel; Joyce and I at our lake home in Texas, where our family, friends, and employees often gather. Of course, I learned a lot about having fun during my college years at Washington State University, where I became a proud, lifelong member of the Sigma Chi fraternity. Yeah, it's okay to have fun.

Cashup loved to have fun, especially at his stage stop and later his hotel. I, too, try to have fun every single day at work; with colleagues, friends, and family; while playing golf; and while completing personal projects. Folks tell me I always have the loudest laugh in the room. I have found that a balance of hard work and play leads to success in life. Takeaway: Cashup had fun.

HARNESS YOUR DRIVE: Restlessness

Cashup was restless. I am, too. When I left the family dairy farm to head to college, I took with me the work ethic instilled by my parents and Future Farmers of America projects and I never looked back. In 1990, I traded my tenured faculty position in meat science at Texas Tech University for the multimedia textbook publishing industry—the original idea of bringing the expert to the classroom—and kept my lifelong secret mentor Cashup with me all the way. I owe him a lot.

PHILANTHROPY: A higher calling

Cashup was the first philanthropist we know of in the Davis family. Yes, he was among the white pioneers who settled on Indian land, but what he did for the Indians in 1878, sending 200 ponies packed with emergency food supplies, was remarkable. Likewise, philanthropy has been a priority for me since 1979. I am especially respectful of the word "perpetuity." That powerful word guides me to this day in all philanthropic decisions for endowments, charitable trusts, and foundations with whom Joyce and I work. With this book about Cashup, it is my hope his story and lessons will live in all of us in perpetuity.

In my public remarks, I often quote this Chinese proverb:

> If you want happiness for one hour—take a nap.
> If you want happiness for a day—go fishing.
> If you want happiness for a year—inherit a fortune.
> If you want happiness for a lifetime—help someone else.

SPIRIT: The soil and the earth

In a letter I wrote to the extended Davis family on July 28, 1989, I said: "I have concluded that Cashup Davis was a true legend in his time who brought joy to people in an era where life was a challenge for all. His wife Mary Ann was a big-hearted realist. Together, they crossed the country, settled in one of the nation's prime agricultural regions, and encouraged others to follow their lead."

It amazes me to this day how Cashup was able to move his family all over the American West—uprooting them on seven occasions—and somehow instinctively know that the Palouse soil under his feet was at the heart of arguably the greatest dryland farm country in the United States.

The spirit spread to my dad Aubrey and his brother Chuck, too, who also loved the Palouse deeply. They experienced much joy driving on Highway 95 through the Palouse countryside, pointing out the owners of various farms and, as all farmers do, admiring the fields, critiquing the various crops, noticing the weeds, assessing their farm equipment, and seemingly knowing the family history of nearly all the farms. I was inspired. They often said wheat farmers on the Palouse only want to buy land that adjoins theirs. But I think most farmers and ranchers say that. They also said low crop prices are not all bad, because it weeds out the weaker farmers. Poppi and Uncle Chuck loved to see excellence in farming.

Cashup's grand vision for a booming Steptoe City never materialized. The town is still there, with a handful of homes, but its restaurant, which had always hung photos of Cashup and the hotel on the walls, closed forever a few years ago. There is a great view of Steptoe Butte from that town.

The land near the old stage stop, where the railroad was built, took on the name "Cashup." Amid the few houses, a giant grain elevator with "Cashup" emblazoned on it rises above the fields and farms. It can be seen for a good distance. That town has an even better view of Steptoe Butte.

And right around the corner from the village of Cashup is Bethel Cemetery, where Cashup and his wife Mary Ann rest side by side, with a large gravestone that stands out from the rest; just as in life, surrounded by their large extended family and a whole lot of other extraordinary homesteading families. All the good people at rest there have the very best view of Steptoe Butte there is.

Someday I will be buried right there near them all—Cashup and Mary Ann, my dad and mom, my brother, and so many other Davises—enjoying that view of Steptoe Butte where the unforgettable luxury hotel opened July 4, 1888, by the one and only Cashup Davis.

View from Steptoe Butte, where the sun breaks through a cloudy afternoon on the Palouse. Photograph by Misty Olsen Photography.

SETTLERS OF THE PALOUSE

Cashup Davis: The "Daniel Boone of the Palouse"

S. D. WOODWARD, PALOUSE SETTLER

"WE'VE GOT ONE—MAYBE TWO—WINTERS LEFT before we lose it," says Greg Partch, long-time leader of the Whitman County Historical Society, pointing at a rustic structure. Winter morning sunshine strikes low on the grasses surrounding it, while orange sunbeams melt off the overnight frost. The streaks of sunshine are also poking through gaping holes in the roof and some of the walls, sending beams straight to the dirt floor of the old pioneer home. This is the one hundred fiftieth winter that the 15-foot by 15-foot homesteaders' house has weathered. It still stands in 2022—tilting ever so slightly. But, as Partch warns, it needs to be saved now or it will be gone. The plaque on the front says, "National Register of Historic Places." John Kelley built it in 1872. Cashup Davis, who lived just a few miles away on the other side of Steptoe Butte, surely walked through its tiny door and peered out its two tiny windows while visiting a neighbor.

How did it survive long enough to become one of the oldest buildings on the Palouse? The answer lies at every corner of the structure. Each hand-hewn log is cut just right so it rests inside hand-cut slots on the opposing log. The building has no vertical beam, because the walls themselves, all cut into each other, are as strong as can be. For sure, it isn't a Lincoln Logs structure—it is the real thing. Kelley was a farmer and rancher, just like almost everyone else who homesteaded on the rolling hills of the Palouse, when he built it. And, like so many others, the Kelley clan still owns and farms the same land.

The word "pioneer" is sometimes used rather casually and can also have negative associations. It is easy to forget the true meaning of the word, especially with regard to the first white settlers on the Palouse. These men and women uprooted their lives and their families, leaving behind their hometowns, friends, and livelihoods. They put everything they owned onto covered wagons, horses, mules, oxen, or their own backs. (The lucky ones got on a train or steamship.) They traveled for weeks or months across prairies that served up severe weather in the form of extreme heat, dust storms, thunderstorms, tornadoes, and snowstorms. They had to bring along provisions while keeping the faith that they would find water along the way. They risked encountering outlaws, Native tribes, or others who, for a variety of reasons, might endanger their lives. Too, if they got sick, they were on their own. Injured? They'd have to make do and stick it out. Many never made it. And for some, getting there was the easy part.

Most immigrants had little idea about what to expect when they arrived. They may have heard about the opportunities in the West from friends or relatives who went before them. Some merely read about it in a newspaper and decided to make the move. Once they arrived, it didn't get any easier. If they wanted to eat, they had to grow food or hunt it. If they wanted shelter, they had to build it. If they wanted land, they had to claim a homestead. If they wanted law and order, they had to cooperate with each other. If they needed help, they had to rely on their neighbors. If they wanted to succeed, they had to work very, very hard. To this day, the American work ethic and the spirit of self-reliance and enterprise is drawn from the pioneers.

Getting around meant walking, riding a horse, or driving a wagon pulled by horses or mules. There were no trains or trucks to haul crops to market. If you bought supplies, you had to haul them from Spokane fifty miles away or from Walla Walla one hundred miles away. As Colfax grew, it provided more stores and services to help supply Whitman County.

People needing medical care, including women in childbirth, had to wait for the doctor to arrive from the nearest town. Formal education came only when neighbors decided to build a school and hire a teacher. Learning was also provided in nearly every home, with books on how to farm, how to take care of a household, how to understand physics, grammar, engineering, geology, and so much more. Fortunate are those descendants of Palouse pioneers whose bookshelves feature scribbles on the inside covers like "1873, to my daughter" or "1877, our family Bible." Books became valuable family possessions, passed from one generation to the next. Many Palouse families have such books now sitting in a place of honor on their shelves. Donna Gwinn, who comes from two Palouse pioneer families and runs the historic McCroskey House Bed and Breakfast in Garfield near the base of Steptoe Butte, has a library full of books that were once owned by her pioneer relatives. Some volumes were carried west over the prairies. Worn but still elegant, they remind us of the intellectual lives of our ancestors. Included are classics of literature: Thomas Malory's tale of King Arthur and the knights of the roundtable, Jane Austen's *Pride and Prejudice*, Sir Walter Scott's *The Talisman*, as well as those penned by Rudyard Kipling, Robert Louis Stevenson, Charles Dickens, Horatio Alger, Geoffrey Chaucer, William Shakespeare, Alfred Tennyson, and many others.

Religion—sometimes very fundamental and severe beliefs—dominated society. The fear of God was almost tangible. Shame was often weaponized. As a matter of priority, churches were sometimes built before schools were built.

Newspapers dotted small towns everywhere, giving a sense of local identity and pride—and some gossip. Truly the first draft of history. Surviving issues provide us with a chronicle of local life and culture.

Drunkenness and lawlessness were not uncommon among the Palouse settlers. And an imperfect justice system struggled to keep the peace.

For better or worse, everyone knew everyone, and families were very important. In time, many folks were related to each other as, with most families having six to twelve children, inevitably some homesteader families married each other.

To name all the leading pioneers of the earliest days of Whitman County and the Palouse would require making judgments about the relative value or visibility of a given family, an impossible task. But the historical record makes it clear they knew they were making history as the first white settlers on the Palouse. And a sense of history was evident whenever newspapers listed the pioneers by the year they arrived on the Palouse. A notation reading "Bradford Holmes, 1876," for example, indicated the year of his arrival on the Palouse. The arrival year sometimes became a sign of a family's status in the community. The sense of history manifested very early on. In 1899, for example, the *Colfax Gazette* listed the pioneers who were still alive and in attendance at a community celebration (they were listed in order of their arrival) under the headline "Plowed Bunch Grass, Some of the Brave Men and Women of Early Palouse Days." That was in 1899, but they viewed the 1870s and 1880s as the "early days." The article says the pioneers "entered a wild, unbroken land and caused it to blossom like a rose." It describes Phillip Brogan, who arrived in 1869, as "proud of the fact that he has lived for 30 years on his Union Flat farm and has not in that time been sick 30 minutes."

The first white person born in Whitman County was Charles E. Ewart, born in 1872 to Capt. and Mrs. James Ewart. They were among the first and most important pioneering families. The 1880 and 1883 Whitman County censuses, likely the first ones conducted, identify the prominent early names: the large Davis family, along with Newmeyer, Stephens, Gwinn, Hughes, Huntley, Matlock, and more.

The Whitman County plat map from 1895 also reveals the names of families who homesteaded the land in the very early days: McGuire, McCroskey, Boyer, Bishop, Hume, Roberts, Kerns, Warren, Cox, O'Dell, Kelley.

Then there are the people who founded Colfax, other small towns, and Whitman County, the ones who established government offices and other community organizations like civic associations, and infrastructure like churches. These civic-minded citizens included the families of Perkins, Cox, Hollingsworth, McCoy, Ewart, Comegya, Bryson, Kennedy, Lucas, Manring, Nosler, Goodyear, Bancroft, Swegle, Elberton, Sproat, Todd, and Neill, among others.

In June 1896, recognizing their roles in the history of the region, the Whitman County Pioneers' Society formed to "keep alive the memory of the brave old days when civilization in the Palouse country was in its earliest youth." Some thirty years on, they wanted to look back on the "brave old days" of pioneer settlement. Its organizers included many of the above names and more: Renshaw, Ringer, Holt, Robbins, and Dowling.

Other pioneer names of note that appeared repeatedly in newspapers, maps, and other literature of the day include LaFollette, Case, Bryson, Logsdon, Kennedy, Hold, Nosler, Hansen, Gulch, Curtis, Schlomer, and Harden.

Back roads laid out during the 1870s and 1880s, tying family farms and farmhouses to the main roads, bear the names of many of these founding families and still dot today's road maps: Hume,

Bancroft, Sienknecht, Baylor, McMeekin, Eckhart, Klemgard, Cashup, and dozens more.

Woefully unheralded pioneer wives followed their husbands into the unknown to find new livelihoods or improve their circumstances. One could not be a pioneer woman without being strong. In the early census records, husbands were often listed as farmers while wives were homemakers, a term honored in 1880 Whitman County, when running a household was like running a survival operation. Laws of the day may have treated them as property of their husbands, but they were every bit as essential as the men in establishing homes and communities.

Miss Leoti L. West, whom we have cited previously with regard to her work as a newspaper reporter, was also revered as "the pioneer school teacher in Colfax"—the first female teacher on the Palouse. West spoke at a fiftieth anniversary of Whitman County pioneer celebration in the summer of 1921.

Mrs. C. G. White was the first white woman "to have her home in Colfax."

The daughter of Capt. and Mrs. James Ewart, true leaders of pioneers, "came to Ewartsville country on Union Flat" with her parents on July 7, 1871. She had two brothers and four sisters. As a young woman, she moved from one established family to another, marrying James A. Perkins, the founder of Colfax and became the unofficial first lady of the biggest town in the county.

We say to Palouse pioneers posthumously, here we are, 150 years after the first of you arrived on the Palouse, and we honor you, we remember your names, and we want the future to know your names. Each name has a story behind it: hardship, reward, self-reliance, work, adventure, and family. Along with the attributes of these pioneers were the values they passed on to their children and their children's children. Indeed, in so many cases, children of the Palouse pioneers carried on these traits. Cashup's family was no exception.

Attendees at the 1925 Pioneers Picnic gather for a photograph. From Northwest Museum of Arts and Culture. Virgil McCroskey Collection, MS 147, Box 2, Folder 8.

Even among the pioneers, there were cliques. Towns had their groups. The farmlands had their groups. As basic survival became less of an issue and formation of society took on greater importance, the divisions began to manifest more distinctly.

Not all pioneers were saints, mind you. And the fathers and husbands were often unreasonably demanding of their families. Cashup was not universally revered, especially by some of the upper crust of town society. He is not always mentioned in the literary writings honoring the leading pioneers of the day. "He wasn't in one of those centers," says Palouse historian Ed Garretson. "He was an entertainer. He knew everybody." And everybody knew him, his jolly ways, his bombastic magniloquence. He threw all-night parties. He did not fit in with the elitism and snobbery of the late 1800s. Cashup built the places where people had fun.

A Celebration of the Pioneers

On November 25, 1921, locals held a celebration of the fiftieth anniversary of the incorporation of Whitman County. But it was really a celebration of the pioneers themselves. Many were still alive and in attendance that day. The *Colfax Gazette* newspaper covered the event, as speaker after speaker stood on a platform under the gazebo to reminisce and reflect, "Henry Chryst told of exploring this part of Whitman County in 1871 and telling his companion that this was the best country he had ever put his head into or ever would and he has not changed his mind."

Among the early settlers was James S. Taylor, who became the first Whitman County sheriff. He built his cabin in March 1871 on Rebel Flat, a couple years before Cashup arrived. "He had crossed the plains to Oregon years before," reported the *Gazette*. A homesteader named Senator Hall "recalled the Colfax postmaster dumping out the mail and calling the names[;] as he sorted it out people watching him would call out, 'Here,' as he read their names." J. S. Klemgard of Pullman said he "was born on the road as his parents were crossing the plains with an ox team." At the celebration that day, Klemgard spoke of "the influence of the pioneers for good" and announced a gift of $100 to start an endowment fund for the use of the Whitman County Pioneers' Association. John Butler of Pine City recalled passing through Colfax as a boy in 1876.

The *St. John Advocate* called S. D. Woodward a "pioneer among pioneers" in a 1912 story. The newspaper noted that he ran a hardware store in nearby Sunset and helped found Whitman County and the *Colfax Gazette*. He even bought the first copy of the newspaper in 1877 for $1.00. "If the county records should ever be destroyed, he could supply a large part of them from his well-stored and retentive memory," the *Advocate* averred. "Among his freshest recollections is the memory of Cashup Davis, the 'Daniel Boone of the Palouse' who built the ranch house now known as the 'St. John House,' which formed the nucleus of our thriving town."

SOURCES

Albany (WA) Register 1 August 1895.

Allen, Karl P., newspaper series in the *Pullman Herald*, 1919.

Becker Paula, "Colfax: Thumbnail History," *HistoryLink.org* (2010).

Bell, O. N., "Reminiscence," *Colville (WA) Examiner* 10 December 1921.

Building The Erie Canal (The History Channel documentary). Rudy Giuliani interview.

"Butler County," *Ohio History and Genealogy* (Cincinnati, Ohio: Western Biographical Publishing, 1882).

Butler (LA) Weekly Times 28 November 1895.

Chase, Mrs. Ivan, "Why Cashup Davis Wanted Grave on Steptoe Butte." *Spokesman-Review* (Spokane, WA) 24 December 1922.

Colfax Gazette, 9 September 1971.

Colfax Gazette, 1911.

Colfax Gazette, 20 July 1900.

Colfax Gazette, June 1896.

Curtis, Mrs. Dale, and Mrs. Edgar Kerns, *Early Pioneers of the Thornton Area*, booklet, 1972.

Cutler, Don, "Your Nations Shall Be Exterminated," *MHQ: The Quarterly Journal of Military History* Spring 2010.

Davis, Grace, handwritten family history.

Eckhart, Julia Davis, handwritten family history.

Encyclopedia Britannica, "Commonwealth vs. Hunt" law case entry.

Evans, Elwood, *History of Pacific Northwest: Oregon and Washington* (North Pacific History Company, 1889).

Gilbert, Frank T. *Historic Sketches of Walla Walla, Whitman, Columbia and Garfield Counties, Washington Territory; and Umatilla County, Oregon* (Portland, OR: Print and Lithographing House of A. G. Walling, 1882).

Greene, Jerome A., "US Army Casualties, Nez Perce War 1877" in *Nez Perce, Summer 1877: The US Army and the Nee-Me-Poo Crisis* (Helena: Montana Historical Society Press, 2000).

Harpole, Chet, letter to Randall Johnson, 30 September 1968.

Hays, Robert G., *A Race at Bay: New York Times Editorials on "the Indian Problem," 1860–1900* (Carbondale: Southern Illinois University Press, 1997).

Johnson, Randall A., *Cashup Davis and His Hotel on Steptoe Butte* (booklet, 1967).

Johnson, Randall, on-camera interview conducted by Gordon Davis, 25 August 2000.

Johnson, Randall, unpublished screenplay concept (1972).

Kentish Gazette 7 November 1843: 3.

Kershner, Jim, "Steptoe Butte Peaked in 1890s," *Spokesman-Review* (Spokane, WA) 26 March 2006.

Koenig, Richard, 2020. Data from "Census of Agriculture."

Kuehl, David G., letter to the *Colfax Gazette*, forwarded to Randall Johnson, 11 February 1972.

Lawhead, Bonita "Cashup built this hotel 40 years too soon," *The Standard Register* (Dayton, OH) Undated.

Lewiston (ID) Teller 7 June 1888.

Mick, Pat, 2020 interview by authors.

Mick, Pat, letter to her great-great-grandmother Mary Ann Davis, written posthumously circa 2010.

"Mount Large Telescope Summit Steptoe Butte; Inland Plans for Entertainment of Tourists," *Lewiston (ID) Evening Teller* 30 September 1908.

New York Evening Post 12 August 1882.

New-York Tribune 27 September 1841.

Northwest Tribune 14 October 1887.

Obituary of James S. (Cashup) Davis, *Colfax (WA) Gazette* June 1896.

Obituary of James S. (Cashup) Davis, *Garfield (WA) Enterprise* 26 June 1896.

Obituary of Mary Ann Davis, *Garfield (WA) Enterprise* October 1894.

Pragnell, Hubert, *Railway Magazine*, April 1838.

Railway Times 5 October 1839.

Rand McNally sectional map of Washington (1890).

"Report from Wilburville," Palouse *Gazette* 13 October 1877.

Roberts, S. C., "Pioneers I Have Known" column, *Colfax Gazette-Commoner*

Shields, L. B. E., D. M. Hunsaker, and J. C. Hunsaker III, "Trends of Suicide in the United States During the 20th Century," in: Tsokos, M. (eds) *Forensic Pathology Reviews*, vol. 3 (Totowa, NJ: Humana Press, 2005).

Shoemaker, Benjamin H. III, letter to Julia Davis Eckhart, 27 March 1963.

Spokane Falls (WA) Review 28 July 1883.

Spokane Falls (WA) Review 20 May 1891.

Spokane Falls (WA) Review 8 May 1892.

St. Clair, Roger, "Earlier Tunnelling on the Kent Coast," in *Back Track* March/April 1994 8(2).

Trafzer, Clifford E. and Richard D. Scheuerman, *Renegade Tribe: The Palouse Indians and the Invasion of the Inland Pacific Northwest* (Pullman: Washington State University Press, 1986)

Unidentified Lewiston, ID-Clarkston, WA newspaper (1968).

Unidentified Spokane, WA newspaper, March 18, 1945.

US Department of State, Office of the Historian https://history.state.gov/

Warner, Deborah Jean, letter mailed to David D. Davis, 4228 E. 10th Avenue, Spokane, WA 99202-5380 on 25 January 1991.

Washington *Standard* 1 June 1888.

Washington State Department of Agriculture, "1918 Biennial Report to Ernest Lister, Governor of Washington, from the Department of Agriculture."

West, Leoti L. interview with Ida Kerns Dennis, *Spokesman-Review* (Spokane, WA) 21 November 1931.

Whitman County Gazette (1890).

Whitman, Marcus, and James K. Kelly, *An Illustrated History of Whitman County, Washington* (San Francisco: W. H. Lever, 1901).

Whitten, David O. "Depression of 1893," *EH.net Encyclopedia*, edited by Robert Whaples. https://eh.net/encyclopedia/the-depression-of-1893/.

Wikipedia, "1841 in the United States" https://en.wikipedia.org/wiki/1841_in_the_United_States

Wikipedia, "History of Immigration to the United States." https://en.wikipedia.org/wiki History_of_immigration _to_the_United_States

ACKNOWLEDGEMENTS
FROM JEFF BURNSIDE

THE RESEARCH AND INVESTIGATION THAT prepared me to write this book went well beyond internet searches to include stepping down creaky stairs and into dusty basements in Eastern Washington small town museums like Tekoa (unofficially curated by Harry Brandt), or Rosalia where the museum sits under lock and key behind the lobby at City Hall. In the town of Palouse, more than 150 years of newspapers are lovingly housed by Janet Barstow in her Printing Press Museum. In Colfax, the still bustling *Whitman County Gazette* operates at the front of the building while 150 years of newspapers are stacked in the back—that is, until they moved it to new quarters recently. In Pullman, a grand archive hidden in a massive closet is protected by historian Ed Garretson. I thank them all.

The role these small-town museums played in this book was, in fact, chronicled in a *Seattle Times Sunday Magazine* cover story I wrote. I thank Magazine Editor Bill Reader, Investigation Editor Jonathan Martin, and Publisher Frank Blethen.

I developed an informal, loose knit team of mostly amateur researchers I called "the Cashup Crew." They each seemed to have a particular expertise—from ship manifests to land claims, cemeteries to agriculture—and helped me track down and verify even the most obscure, hard to find facts about Cashup's world. The team includes Whitman County Historical Society President Greg Partch, St. John Historical Society chief Lydia Smith,

Cashup descendants John Rupp and Linda Banken, genealogist Claudia Broderson, McCroskey House Innkeeper Donna Gwinn (from two pioneer families), history sleuth Sharon Hall, agriculture titan Alex McGregor, lawyer Rusty McGuire, Linda and Lee McGuire who now live in the home built by Cashup's son Charley, author Richard Scheuerman, and the members of two other pioneer families Nick Manring and Jim Gisselberg. Linda Bathgate, my editor at Washington State University Press and its plucky new boutique subsidiary Basalt Books, made my manuscript cleaner and better. Thanks.

Standing apart from them all is Jim Martin, descended from Cashup's family, specifically Cashup's wife Mary Ann Martin (Davis). Jim had already been investigating Davis family letters and lovingly restoring family photos, including many of those you see in this book. We call him our Chief Consulting Historian. Best of all, Jim is the spitting image of Cashup himself. As of this writing, we hope to get Jim on a stage for a one-man show about Cashup.

After years as a television news investigative reporter, it was great fun to turn my sights to writing a book. I believe it is meticulously researched but I look forward to having some of the old-timers of the Palouse point out errors—tiny ones, I hope. That you have purchased and are reading this book means more to me than all the Emmys and honors I've received during my career. I hope I've pleased my incredible mentors from my formative years at KING TV Seattle who took me under their wings, especially indomitable reporter Julie Blacklow.

I want to express great gratitude to the Ted Scripps Environmental Journalism Fellowship that I was awarded in 2017. My year in advanced journalism study at the University of Colorado in Boulder laid the groundwork for taking on such a book project. As of this writing, we are nearly finished with the documentary film that parallels this book. It is the same story but with strong emotion and cinematography in a very different story-telling platform. I live comfortably in both the written and broadcast journalism worlds. As part of the Scripps Fellowship, special thanks go to my friend and fellow journalist Tom Yulsman, the Executive Director of the Center for Environmental Journalism; legendary law professor Charles Wilkinson; Liz Carter, President of the Scripps Howard Foundation; and Cindy Scripps Leising, Ted Scripps' daughter.

I first met Gordy Davis during a campaign to build a new Sigma Chi Fraternity house at Washington State University. He kept talking about this incredible guy named Cashup. I said "Gordy, you should write a book about Cashup." He said "well, you need to write it with me." And we did. He's become a good friend and I've learned a great deal about Gordy and about the world through him. I tried to accurately reflect Gordy's voice in writing these pages. He's a cigar-chomping, colorful Alpha male with a gigantic heart. In our interviews about Cashup and how their lives intertwined, Gordy would tear up. "Ol' Gordo", as he sometimes calls himself, is a fine, fine man.

Finally, to anyone who knows me, it should be no surprise that I am deeply grateful to the love and unfailing support of my beautiful wife Carole McDowell Burnside. I am so fortunate to have her in my life. Thank you.

ACKNOWLEDGEMENTS
FROM GORDON DAVIS

I WOULD LIKE TO ACKNOWLEDGE the following, without whom the story of Cashup would have never come to life:

My wife, Joyce Davis—thanks for your patience, love, and understanding as I've worked on this project the past three years. Your endless support of my crazy ideas and relentless pursuits never goes unnoticed—I love you, honey.

Jeff Burnside—thank you for selling me on the idea to create an insightful nonfiction book about my beloved great-grandfather, and for sharing his story honestly and beautifully. You're a world-class investigator, writer, and friend. Thank you for ALL the hard work you've poured into seeking the truth and conveying Cashup's essence and legacy—my beloved Secret Mentor.

Linda Bathgate—you're an absolute pro. Thank you for your advice, candid feedback, and guidance, recruiting reviewers, and coaching of a couple of rookies. We wouldn't have gotten to the finish line, on time and according to plan, without you!

Elizabeth Chilton—for not only writing a testimonial but also a stunning foreword for this project—and on short notice—wow! You are a dear friend and I cherish your wisdom and moxie.

Rich Koenig—a noteworthy WSU soil scientist, thanks to you and your Cougar academic team for examining the census of agriculture records within a 50-mile radius of the butte and estimating the dollar value of all livestock and crops over time. Your work illustrated reality to the vision Cashup shared about the potential productivity of the view from his telescope in 1888.

Jim Martin—my cousin and close look-alike to Cashup himself, and collector of much historical information about the Davis family, and Cashup in particular. Thank you for your loyalty and insight throughout this project.

Matt Owens—thanks for being my Chief of Stuff, for all the tasks and coordination you've managed, and for the advice and dedication you've given to getting our book to press on time.

Sincere gratitude to Mike Leach, Lawrence Schovanec, Tom Yulsman, Rob Angel, Gerald and Tricia Posner, David Baron and Kevin Pond for taking the time to read our book and provide testimonials. Your friendship and support mean the world to me.

And finally, many thanks to the entire Cashup Crew who spent time digging through attics and sharing materials, history, and anecdotes for our project. Your passion is inspirational and the content you brought to light is paramount to telling the true story of the one and only Cashup Davis.

ABOUT THE AUTHORS

JEFF BURNSIDE IS AN ACCOM-PLISHED investigative reporter with several dozen national, regional, and local honors for reporting and philanthropy, including ten regional Emmy awards for his television news reporting. His work has fueled new laws in multiple states and municipalities, triggered the return of millions of dollars to consumers and taxpayers, helped inspire a U.S. Supreme Court case that changed White House policy on Navy training, and aided in putting numerous unscrupulous people behind bars. His work has taken him to the top of mountains and to the bottom of the sea, to all fifty states and more than two dozen nations. Jeff is the recipient of a 2017 Ted Scripps Fellowship in Environmental Journalism at the Center for Environmental Reporting at the University of Colorado in Boulder. He is also past president of the Society of Environmental Journalists. He serves on a number of nonprofit boards and national journalism judging panels. His journalistic work now is authoring books and producing documentary films, living comfortably in text and broadcast: this book will also be a documentary film. Jeff also proudly serves the Sigma Chi Foundation raising funds for scholarships and leadership training. He and his wife Carole live near Seattle, Washington.

Raised on wheat and dairy farms in Washington, GORDON W. DAVIS has been involved in education for fifty-three years. As iCEV chairman, Davis was the executive producer of more than two thousand educational productions until selling his company in 2021 and turning fully toward philanthropy, plus having fun. He has authored or co-authored thirty-six refereed scientific journal articles and ninety-three meat science publications. He co-coached two national championship university meat-judging teams and has founded or co-founded fifteen endowments and one foundation, with three college or building namings in his honor. Since 1964, Davis has received forty-nine industry, university, and business awards, including national awards from the Association of Career and Technical Education; National Agricultural Alumni Association; the USDA; FFA; Sigma Chi fraternity; US Chamber of Commerce; and the American Meat Science Association. He earned two bachelor of science degrees from Washington State University and a masters and Ph.D. from Texas A&M University. He also worked as a meat scientist for thirteen years at the University of Tennessee and Texas Tech University.